Re-Wired: Finding Faith Through the Challenges of Stroke

Kym Kennedy

ISBN-13: 978-1-7782205-3-1

Cover design by: Lexy Kennedy

Edited by: Michael Brodie

For my daughter... and for those who struggle to find peace and meaning after stroke. You are not alone.

Introduction

I've learned something about human nature. If you put a new Adam and Eve in the garden, and tell them all of the stories of the first Adam and Eve, though it might take her a while longer, the new Eve would still bite the apple, and the new Adam would eventually join in. We're flawed. Despite knowing better, and despite the overwhelming guilt that follows, try as we might for perfection, we're never going to be God. We're always going to need God, and we're too damned stubborn to just accept that as reality. We condemn ourselves to worries we don't have to bear, responsibilities we don't need to take on, and the inevitable messes we create by telling ourselves that we can control things that we can't. That's me in a nutshell; an apple-biting glutton for punishment. And yet, God still loves me.

Perhaps it's as simple as the "glass half full or empty" argument. When tragedy strikes, there are those who blame God for allowing it to happen, and those who look for the lessons and motivation it was meant to spark. I'm so incredibly grateful to be among the latter.

I had a stroke, and I'm still here. I lost such valuable skills and talents, but I've seen them mercifully restored to me one at a time. Clearly, God has purpose for both me and my skills. I can write. I can express myself with a measure of depth and clarity, and I've lived unique experiences with the perspective of a solitary mind. I belong within pages, helping misunderstood people to find their words. I don't claim wisdom. I think it would be quite unwise to do so. But I can absolutely claim God's direction, as I pray for the words to make a difference, and to do so to His glory.

I feel like it's indicative of an ill society that the brightest among us would rather aspire to be rocket scientists than prophets. We don't pursue the meaning of life in the vigorous way earlier generations have. Perhaps our surroundings lack the inspiration to do so, as we try to accept social media philosophers absent of accountability, and blind adherence to social constructions as a way of life. I've been granted the gift of a second chance to seek what is meaningful. Herein lies that exploration.

Your Purpose

The skills and talents that you have; the gifts that God bestows,
Abilities you find within, uniquely yours to know.
Within those things, your purpose lies, important, deep and great.
Embrace the things that form your life; the emblems of your fate.

For in acceptance of your path, though burdened, sad and strained,
Lies knowledge, truth and deeper faith, in all that's unrestrained.
With reason, you were put here, and for purpose, you remain.

∞∞∞

Forty-six years old. That doesn't seem like the right age to have a stroke. Strokes are supposed to happen when you're in your nineties, about five years after your health visibly declines, and three years after people start whispering when they think you're out of earshot, that you've lived a full life. I was just starting to complain that my body doesn't move like it did when I was twenty. Old enough to want to stop for a breather between roller coasters at the amusement park, but young enough to still have the "Vomit Comet" on my bucket list.

I still can't fully grasp the seriousness and effect of a stroke on my life and my future. What I do grasp fully is that all that I believed was mine to control in this lifetime, is an illusion. God decided the very moment that I would enter this world, and He'll decide when and how I leave it. The gifts and talents that I have can be taken or grown exponentially at His behest, at any time. Every breath is bestowed by my Creator, and in the moments that I find the courage to surrender to that knowledge, I'm not terrified. I'm free. It's a funny thing to feel the utter certainty in the pointlessness of stress amidst the reality that you control nothing. A weightlessness that is quested after like a Holy Grail, that human nature won't seem to allow us to grasp with the commitment due to the enlightenment it could give. There's no point in worry when God is in control. My favourite verse from scripture is "Trust in the Lord with all your heart and lean not on your own understanding; in all your ways acknowledge Him, and

He shall direct your paths." (Proverbs 3:5-6, NKJ version) I remind myself of the importance of that message almost every day now. If only I could submit fully to what I know to be true. Accept that God is in control and praise Him for the blessings He bestows. Why is that so difficult?

I never realized how much I took for granted. Phenomenal skills I used poorly, a unique mind that I rarely shared with others, and a knowledge of God's presence absent of the motivation to try to know Him better. In an instant, I lost so much. In truth, through honest self-reflection, I lost what I never proved worthy of in the forty-six years I had to try. As I regained those skills and abilities one at a time, I committed to not taking them for granted again. The gifts that God gives come with a duty to use them to His glory. In this, even those who are non-believers benefit from the altruistic motivations of God's people. And yet… what a challenge it is to attempt the perfection of faith from the imperfect form of humanity. In facing that challenge, I shall never stop striving.

Renewed

It's not some romantic story,
Where I lay in bed and convalesce until that miraculous moment, when I rise in perfect voice and declare my mind healed, and my lips unrestrained from confusion.

I want to ball up simple writing like the trash it comes out as.

I quiet my inner screams over stuttered words.

Inside, a silent tantrum over a missing word, like a child who stubs his toe, and angrily kicks the object out of his way.

To be embarrassed by the simplicity of work and the challenge it presents to me, while being grateful for my ability to rise to it.

My conviction will place my feet firmly on the ground.

Each word I put to paper, or articulate against the odds, builds my core.

My child motivates me.

My frustration challenges me.

My God renews me, until I convalesce no more.

I vividly remember the moment that my nephew and my mother found me in bed, shortly after my stroke. It was the first time I tried to open my mouth and articulate what I had experienced. I hadn't tried to speak before that. That's when I knew. I remember looking into my mother's eyes, desperate and panicked. I had been sick, but regardless of how long that pesky bug was lingering, I was destined to eventually recover fully. Of course I would. Just as I had done countless times before. But, in that moment, that certainty vanished, and I was terrified. My daughter was at school. My daughter! I'm a single mother, and my world came crashing down. The world that supports her and aspires to lift her up.

Sometimes, when I lay in bed, I look to my left and can still see my mother's concerned face looking back at me. I can still see the immediate look of determination on my nephew's face, to fix the problem or right the wrong. I can still feel the mental desolation that overcame me. But I don't think that the memories are the curse they sound like.

Remembering the panic makes me grateful for God's peace. Remembering the desperation of loss makes me feel so powerful in my recovery. Remembering the crippling fear of not being capable for my child makes our life together such a remarkable blessing. I want to remember. I never want to have to learn those lessons again.

Fear Not

Panicked, shattered, filled with fear.
Overwhelmed, I shed a tear.
Lost inside myself, not knowing,
How to stop despair from growing.

Help me! Give me all the answers.
Grasping hard for second chances.
"Is this my future?" I scream inside.
A prospect I cannot abide.

The words won't come; no way to tell,
How fast and hard my spirit fell.
I can't cry out. I can't explain,
The depth of trauma, fear and pain.

Then came a voice that stilled my fright.
"Fear not, My child. I'll make it right."

∞∞∞

One would think that at the age of forty-six, a trip to the hospital that resulted in a stroke diagnosis, would be shocking for the patient. For me, it was quite the opposite.

I had been ill for a month with whatever the virus was that was going around at the time. Congestion, vomiting, a horrible cough, body ache... the range of usual symptoms. I found myself taking substantially more NyQuil or Buckley's than the package recommended. I also used Cannabis to sleep at night, which had become common practice for me. When that month of illness seemed to be wrapping up, I thought it prudent to try to rid my body of excess medication, and I made the choice to stop all forms of medication completely. It was extremely hard on my body, to a very surprising extent.

For ten days, I couldn't consume more than a hundred calories per day or sleep more than an hour a night. I assumed my body was being overly sensitive to withdrawal, and that the near-torture I was putting myself through, would result in a clean body, devoid of drug or illness. By day seven, I had lost my voice, but I had read that withdrawal improves after a week, so I pressed on. On day ten, I tried to get up from my chair to move to my bed, and I dropped to the floor in confusion and disorientation. While it was difficult to fathom a stroke at forty-six, I couldn't speak clearly. I tried to communicate thoughts in my whisper, and the words were jumbled, or just not there. When I wanted to say something, I had to close my eyes, picture the word that I wanted to say, and then sound it out, occasionally having to remind myself of what sound a letter made. I attempted to write my thought, and my pen ran in scribbles off the page. I was lost in my own head, and I couldn't fathom what could have happened to me other than a stroke. My mother and nephew came to check on me, and I managed to convey "I think I've had a stroke," and they took me to the hospital.

It turned out that what I thought was just withdrawal symptoms, was a mix of withdrawal and aspirated pneumonia. Upon arrival at the Emergency Room, I once again managed to whisper, "I think I've had a stroke." The nurse tested my resistance and co-ordination in my hands and legs, which seemed normal, recognized my other very visible symptoms, and saw only the pneumonia. When the doctor got to me, I said again "I think I've had a stroke." He too tested my physical abilities, and expressed no concern, but admitted me for the pneumonia that seemed quite serious. Every medical professional I could reach with the sound of my whisper, I told "I think I've had a stroke," and when none seemed to take it seriously within the many hours I was there, I checked myself out against doctors' orders. That's not something I would have done with a clear mind, but I didn't have that. I had confusion and frustration and fear. Within twenty-four hours, I realized the danger in having left, and I returned to the hospital, where I was admitted for about two weeks.

When I returned to the hospital, I resumed my efforts of trying to get someone... anyone... to understand how far away I was from who I knew myself to be. My mind was scrambled. My speech wouldn't align with my thoughts. My writing was unrecognizable. Nurses and doctors would steadily flow in and out of my room for long enough to ask random questions, but not long enough for my mind and tongue to co-ordinate answers of any value. It was about four days into my hospital stay that the doctor came in, I began to cry, and still with nothing more than a whisper, I said to her "You have to listen to me. I've had a stroke." Once again, she tested my resistance and co-ordination, and through my tears, I repeated "You have to listen. I've had a stroke." She looked at me and agreed to send me for a brain scan later that day.

The next morning, the nurse came in, drew more blood than I knew I had, and a new doctor came in, however briefly, to tell me that I'd be hearing from the physiotherapist and the speech therapist. I asked what my brain scan had shown, and he casually said that it was a stroke. Two spots in the pre-frontal cortex. He left the room twenty seconds later, as if my world hadn't fallen apart. As if it hadn't taken me days to get through to them. As if a stroke at forty-six years old, is a casual occurrence. It wasn't a shock to me. I knew what had happened and felt a modicum of comfort in finally having a diagnosis. But it seemed to surprise them more than anticipated, and it felt as though they were distancing themselves from culpability.

Listen

Listen to the words I speak,
Though my mind and voice seem weak.
I'm stuck inside this shell of me.
Frustration builds, and you don't see.

Your patience with my progress, slow.
From where I came, you do not know.

My mind, alive, sparks flying bright,
And lit up eyes with deep insight.

Listen, as I scream inside.
This isn't me; my tongue is tied.
My brain, confused, I'm feeling lost.
I'm sorting words my mind has crossed.

Listen! If you do not hear,
I don't know where I'll go from here.

∞∞∞

Unless you live in a tightly knit community, when you walk into a hospital, the people providing care have no basis of comparison for how you normally present. You may be sullen by nature. You might be prone to over-exaggeration. It's possible that you're just quiet. I didn't have the voice to convey how far I was from myself.

I wonder if they'd even recognize me now; months later. Would they have a sudden understanding of why I struggled so desperately? Could they recognize how far I've come? Would curiosity strike them over how far I might still have to go?

Perhaps they weren't meant to know who I once was. But, by God's mercy, I will show them who I'm meant to be. At the extension of their helping hand, they will see me rise, spectacularly.

Forever Me

My thoughts and fancies intertwine,
In clusters of a web designed,
Of intricacies so refined,
You'll never sort my stunning mind.

For in it, not just wild tales,
Heroic wins and epic fails,
The fruitful prize of great travails,
Or boisterous wind that fills my sails.

Beyond the memories of a past,
That built a spirit poised to last,
A life so elegantly cast,
It answers questions never asked.

How could you know what forms the chain,
Of tear-filled joy from heartfelt pain,
Amassing in a sweet refrain,
Of hope and beauty that remain.

Unique and still in conscious thought,
Blessed with faith through wars long fought,
Ever-changing as I'm taught,
Remade of facets long forgot.

It has proven to be both a curse and a blessing to have been through a stroke at a relatively young age. Though not thrilled by the prospect of being on blood thinners and cholesterol medication for the rest of my life, the speed at which I've managed to recover is absolute proof of miracles. When the stroke first happened, I was terrified. I had no cause to be well-versed in the afflictions and potential recovery of those who suffered from it. As far as I knew, all that I had lost, might never return.

So much of my life was focused on communication. My most recent path had been initiated by a book that I wrote. It led to deep conversations with brilliant intellectual minds, and speaking engagements with a friend and mentor who allowed me to tag along on her whirlwind journey and learn from her how to give a voice to those who couldn't find their own.

At home, I'm a single mother to a teenaged girl, who I've raised on the importance and promise of communication. Though I often don't have the answers to life's deep and meaningful questions, I've always had the ability to admit my shortcomings and talk through them to new understanding. What if I couldn't write again, or speak clearly again? What if I couldn't be what my daughter needed me to be? As I laid there with my jumbled mind torturing me with threats of no future, the clarity of a single thought shone brightly through the confusion. God is in control, and I'm still here for a reason.

When I was young and largely misunderstood by others, I started writing poetry. I could sort out my thoughts and feelings in the rhythm and flowery words that carried meaning in both their definition and their unique use. As I laid there in the hospital, I reached for the pad of paper and pen that was on the table next to me. I tried to write my name. Then I tried again. Then I very slowly tried to write "The quick brown fox jumped over the lazy sleeping dog." When I say, "very slowly," I mean with tears and twenty-minute long pauses every few words. It was an absolute mess, and it frustrated me beyond measure. But, in the end, there on my page, was every letter in the English language. And while the sight of the unfamiliar scribbles reduced me to tears, I did recognize every letter.

The next sentence that I attempted to write, wasn't a manufactured practice tool. It was an expression of my mind. With words out of place, and awkward vocabulary choices, I was exhausted by my seemingly unsuccessful attempt, but I could see pieces of what I was trying to say, so I continued. My painfully slow writing attempts became like puzzles, and I would spend hours trying to decode and reorganize my mind on paper. The hospital speech therapist saw my attempts and cheered me on.

After only a week and a half in hospital, with both effort and prayer, I looked down at my deciphered page and saw the first glimpse of myself. In terrible handwriting, there was written a poem, familiar to my spirit, equal to my heart, and brilliant in the part of my mind that God had blessed me with the gift of restoring.

Fragments

I'm lost inside myself; scattered pieces that make up who I used to be. Language was my art, and it flowed like velvety colours of curiosity and sparked introspection.

Now, wires that fray into oblivion and bold thoughts that go nowhere, dangle in front of me, teasing me to reach for them.

Frustrated, but not defeated. I am lifted up by the Creator. I am motivated by a daughter. I am blessed with a phenomenal foundation of people that raise me up and will hold me there until their arms break.

With them, I will reconnect each tiny thread and find purpose in the journey. I am a puzzle, with many facets and unexplored perspectives. Wait until you see what God makes of me next.

From fragments to mosaic. By my Creator, I will be created once again.

∞∞∞

Even after significant recovery after a stroke, everything you attempt to do for the first time is scary. Can I walk around my block without collapsing? Can I swallow solid foods without aspirating? Can I still drive a car? I've felt my pulse in my neck before, but suddenly I wonder if every twitch, gasp or twinge is life threatening. I'm acutely aware of quirks that have eluded me for a lifetime.

I've always been a little adventurous. I'm not athletic to any extent, so when I run off of a beach to go parasailing, it looks like a lazy, disoriented elephant trying to take flight. But I still enjoy the excitement of new experiences. I wonder if I can still seek thrills?

While still early in my recovery, my voice is still strained, sore and raspy. By nighttime, it cuts out and threatens to disappear completely. Though I've always struggled with energy levels, when I take on the challenge of an afternoon outing, or remain busy throughout the day, by bedtime, I can't hold my head up and I feel like my eyes are moving independently of each other. I recognize how incredibly fortunate I am to be able to engage in those activities at all. I'm beyond blessed. But the question still rages in my mind "How much of who I've always been, has been lost forever?"

The Fire in Your Eyes

The magic of the spark that illuminates the eyes,
Of someone with an active mind, discriminately wise,
The twinkle that can speak a word that lets you know one better;
The active thoughts you see take shape, in a mind that is unfettered.

When I look in the mirror now, I don't know who I see.
My face, the same, my eyes, still green, but missing what is me.
I stare with slight confusion, mourning who I used to be,
Even as I hope, through journey, with a new soliloquy.

It's only human that we fear a future that's unknown.
Through introspection, deep in heart, in everything I own,
I'm certain that my faith in God has meaningfully grown,
And life can only flourish more, when Christ becomes your home.

So, as I stare at my reflection, and try to find that light,
That sparkled deep behind my eyes; a glint that shone so bright,
I'll look a little deeper, and may God bless me with the sight,
To forget about the spark and see the fire that He lights.

I had never experienced anxiety or claustrophobia on any meaningful level before. I knew what random panic over events or threats felt like, but ongoing affliction of those feelings, was new to me after my stroke.

For the first ten days that I was in hospital, I was moderately quarantined. I could still have visitors in masks and gowns but was alone for much of the time. I'm certain that loneliness contributed to my new challenges. It's a dangerous thing to be left alone with your thoughts, when your thoughts are all unorganized words and confusion. I wasn't in any condition to do a scholarly dive into the effects of stroke and the likelihood of recovery. I just marinated in fear and disorder.

Strange as it might sound, in my exploration of my surroundings, I spotted a shape among the spots on the floor, that looked like a bunny. Ordinarily, it's not something I'd have noticed. But with nothing to do and no one around, I became acutely aware of my surroundings.

My daughter once had a bunny, and I came to love her. She was cute and fluffy, with a playful personality, and more attitude than I knew a bunny could have. When I looked at that spot on the floor, I would think of her, and my mind would settle. The thoughts were familiar and brought home a little bit closer.

Unfortunately, there was no bunny spot to help me overcome my new feelings of claustrophobia. Perhaps it was the presence of pneumonia and oxygen tubes that made me panic over face masks. But, when they made me wear one, locked my head into position, and put me into an MRI machine for a half hour long test, I was quietly traumatized in a way that I still feel now.

I wish that I could claim that I prayed, put my faith in God, and found peace. But that wasn't what happened at all. I wept inside of myself. I panicked at my fate. I counted the seconds until it ended. I was entirely lost and afraid, in my new claustrophobia.

When I returned home from the hospital, I hadn't recovered from that experience. My bedroom is in the basement of my house, and I've always used blackout curtains to make sleeping more comfortable. "Comfort" is not what I found upon my return, and I couldn't sleep in that room. For about a week, I slept in the living room, looking out the large front window, that I'd open a bit, even amidst brisk temperatures.

It seems as though, the greater the challenge, the harder it is to commit it to God's grace, and the harder one falls into chaos.

Thankfully, the comfort of home, and the time for reflection as I looked out my living room window, gave pause to my panic. God had guided me in all else since my stroke, and in a clear moment, He gave me the strength to trust in Him for this challenge too.

When Walls Close In

Trapped inside my panicked mind,
The gruesome images I find,
Of shadows that my demons cast,
In empty darkness, deep and vast.

A fear that overcame me so,
Despite the power that I know,
My Saviour could alleviate,

As closing walls would not abate.

Inside my prison, I remained,
My mind entrenched, my soul in pain,
Until I found the faith I'd lost,
And felt the lonely, pointless cost.

My God grants peace, when in my heart,
I recognize His healing part.

∞∞∞

Emotions are a funny thing. They must be. Since my stroke, I laugh at myself for the things I cry over. It's absurd, amusing, and confounding. Clearly, the emotional centre of my brain hasn't properly re-wired.

I enjoy watching the television show "The Big Bang Theory." When I was in hospital, I had my portable DVD player with me, and a few seasons of the show on disc, to occupy my mind and my free time. It took me about half a dozen episodes to realize that every one of them had made me cry. Apparently, Sheldon Cooper's quirks had become a deep tragedy, and emotional moments between characters warranted full-on sobbing. Had I not been able to laugh at myself for that, I'd have been worried.

It's an element of my life that I think I'm going to have to cope with long-term; dramatic reactions and wild feelings over simplistic things. It's not the norm for me, and it gives me new sympathy for those who struggle with emotional outbursts regularly.

I've always viewed the real challenge of being a woman, as understanding and mastering the emotions introduced to you throughout your life at various stages. As a child, it was things like jealousy, the introductions of love, and the frustrations of limitations. In my teens, it was the warm and fuzzy feelings brought on by hormonal fluctuations and the anger induced by adult problems. The neuropathways I've spent a lifetime creating, are tattered and frayed, and as a forty-six-year-old woman, I feel like I'm starting again, albeit with a large head start, at re-establishing my emotional female prowess.

I wonder why God would present me with that challenge? Did I get it wrong the first time? Am I meant to better understand those who struggle similarly? Does it make room for new emotions that guide my purpose more meaningfully? I suspect that the answer to all of these things is "yes," as I watch for the lessons and pray for the answers.

Outbursts

"Take a breath," I tell myself, as I'm accosted by irrational reactions.

How do I clear the fog? The condensation formed when compassion collides with the ultimate force of being drastically overwhelmed?

"Get a grip!" I deeply chide.
I cover up my face and hide,
Embarrassed by what's found inside;

A passion logic can't abide.

Emotions that I once controlled,
Stirring drama, long untold,
And out I burst in tears and pain,
Until I find myself again.

∞∞∞

I got out of hospital at the beginning of November. For all intents and purposes, the launch of the Christmas season in Canada. Our stores overflow with red and green from the moment they open on November 1st, and holiday markets and events begin on the very first weekend after Halloween.

I'm that embarrassing gal that exists in every group. I'm the one who wears the Santa hat and has lights hidden throughout my furry white jacket that blink to the festive musical switch that's in my pocket. I go to all the Christmas markets and invest large sums of money in Buttercrunch, fudge and shortbread, and whatever other festive treats look like they'll cause heart attacks and tooth decay. The amount of chocolate dipped fruit that I consume throughout the season would concern even the most liberal sweet eater. Or, at least, that's how it used to be.

I don't think that it's a bad thing that I've lost my taste for sweets, per se. It's just so strange. I'm not longing for the urges of gluttony, but I am stopping at all the same vendors as in previous years and then questioning why I'm there. One of my two favourite tastes in all the world, was chocolate covered strawberries, and when I put one in my mouth, I (discreetly) spit it back out again.

It's just another way that I'm getting to know myself all over again. My tastes. My likes and dislikes. My limits, both physically and mentally.

I have incredibly supportive people around me, who I'm very thankful to have. The most common reassurance that I'm offered, amidst my remarkable recovery, is that "it will all come back, eventually." I happily accept the comment in the spirit in which it's intended. But the truth is, they're wrong. There are parts of me that are fundamentally changed, new challenges that I'm highly likely to continue to face for a lifetime, and a call to grace that was so loud, I pray that it rings through my ears for an eternity. I will never again be who I was. But I can be someone better.

The Chance to Be a Better Me

I do not mourn,
What I have lost.
For I'm reborn,
On roads I've crossed.
The heart I knew,
And values set,
I cling to few,
With no regret.

For I am but a slate, untouched;
A screaming soul that has been hushed.
A tablet for God's awesome art,
Fresh and clean in mind and heart.

I'm made of hope.

I am the chance,
To grow the scope,
Of faithful dance.
Of colours bright,
And rhythm new,
On me He writes,
All that is true.

∞∞∞

On my first trip to see my doctor, after having been released from the hospital, the first thing she said to me was "I see you're really catching up on unused Ontario Health Insurance spending." I hadn't been to her office in a few years, and she was shocked to see me at her doorstep under the circumstances that took me there.

From the moment doctors realized that I had indeed suffered a stroke, the action taken on my part was noteworthy. In hospital, I had MRI, ultrasound, x-rays, an obscene amount of blood draws, and visits from physiotherapists and a speech therapist. Upon release, there were more blood requisitions, further ultrasounds, outpatient speech therapy, and referral to a Stroke Clinic. In Canada, achieving all those things within a few months, is indicative of how seriously they view your condition. While frustrated by how long it took to get them to perform the test necessary to diagnose my stroke, I was incredibly grateful for the care that came after. I remain incredibly grateful for the care that continues.

I've questioned how much faith I'm supposed to have in doctors, and how much I'm supposed to commit to God alone. I remembered the parable that I was told years ago about the man drowning at sea, crying out to God for help and committing to the faith that God would save him. Three times, boats approached him, and men extended their arms to rescue him, and he declined, declaring that God would save him. The man drowns, and upon arrival at the Pearly Gates, he asked Saint Peter why God didn't save him, and Saint Peter responded "He sent three boats! What more did you want?" Through recollection of that story, I determined, my doctor is my boat, and I hopped on board.

Grateful

I'll be forever grateful, for the blessings people share,
And the knowledge, to my benefit, from those providing care.
I feel how truly thankful I am, within my heart,
For the gracious work of others, that set my path apart.

I'm strong in body and in mind,
Because of souls that were so kind,
Who led the way when I was blind.

God set these angels in my path,
Of nature, soul and allopath.

Never could my heart express,
With gratitude, through my distress,
For all they gave, I'm truly blessed.

∞∞∞

When will I learn to look at pictures; reflections of my past, and not reminisce about "the last time I was whole?" I honestly recognize the many things in my life that have changed for the better. I value my new-found passion for faith more than words can say. I fully believe in the opportunity to become a better, more valuable person. So why do I look at photos of my daughter and me, prior to my stroke, and think like that?

Maybe what I truly mean is "the last time I knew myself," or "the last time I recognized my limits." There's no path back to where I was before. Recovery doesn't mean that the parts of my brain that were deprived of oxygen too long to survive, suddenly come back to life. It means that God created such a miraculous system that we can develop new pathways, restore and rebuild, and soldier on as something new. There are no guarantees that "new" will mean "better." New challenges don't come with the assurance of success, and we're prone to the same human nature that we've always had.

I think that, throughout life, we develop strategies that allow us to cope with our flaws; stories and excuses that make it possible to live with ourselves. That's what makes life-changing events so terrifying. What if I face the flaws in the new me, and just can't accept them? What if my child can't, and I don't have a good enough story or excuse to give her comfort?

"The last time I was whole" doesn't mean that I was wholly satisfied, whole in perfect purpose, or whole in depth and understanding. It means that a brain I didn't use to its potential lit up fully, amidst the abilities I took for granted. As the adage goes... The lights were on, with nobody home. "The last time I was whole" was the last time I skated by on confident appearance, and "just enough" knowledge to feign meaning.

I don't long to return to the photographs. I long for the commitment to my God, and the confidence in my worthiness of His mercy, to look at new photographs, not in search of "the last time I was whole," but in tearful joy of "the first time I was His."

Artistry

Perhaps it is through vanity, I knew my face so well.
The height of my brow,
The curve of my lip,
The depth and brightness that sprang from my eyes, as more than just familiarity of colour, but as understanding of the hues that formed it.

Subtle changes,
Not observed by those around me.
Absent of the joys that made me smile...
A glint that indicated happiness...
A downturned mouth denying me the memory of what satisfaction once looked like.

Am I still there?
The colours and hues have changed.

I still know what I knew before.
Love and understanding are still mine.

The Master Artist molds my lines and mixes my tones.
From Him, I am become Art;
A magical canvas, not meant to show the world the uniqueness and beauty of a familiar face,
But to show me the world,
To paint my part in it and show me what a phenomenal thing it could be.

∞∞∞

Just when you think it's safe to define the new parameters of your life…

The consequences of stroke are a little bit different than other physical events. Though tragic in its onset, sometimes new symptoms present, weeks, or even months later. When you think you're in the clear, with nothing but improvement ahead, your brain or body throws another curveball, and you're faced with the challenge of incorporating another inconvenience into your life.

It was just shy of two months after my stroke, when I was quizzically looking at a small black spot on my wall from across the room, wondering what it was and when it appeared there. It only took a moment to realize that it was a figment, and it appeared there when my brain confused the signal sent from my optic nerve. It happened a few times that day, and then a few times the next day. A shiny new quirk, that reduced me to tears before I prayed for strength and guidance and tried to open myself to a new understanding of the struggles of others. When I'm tired, it happens more, and often the remedy is as simple as changing my line of sight or adjusting the lighting.

There is a unique fear that accompanies the psychological symptoms of stroke. Studies, that I wish I had never read, describe the increased potential for dementia and the likelihood of depression or anxiety. Fears that test your faith. A faith that I'm determined will win out, as God directs my path, with reason for everything.

God put this array of emotions in us, with purpose. It's okay to have fears when they guide you to Him. But if you confront those fears without faith, it's possible that they will consume you. Curiosity that makes you question your direction and purpose, can propel you forward, while questions like "why me?" will only drive despair. Embrace the spectrum of what you feel with God's presence in your life and know that the spots on the wall will either fade, or become images of art, bold in what they portray.

The Light

My mind plays tricks.
What my eyes perceive, my soul questions.

Am I deceived by illusions, or enlightened by images I'm not yet wise enough to interpret?

Show me what I'm meant to know, in pictures I was never meant to see.

Compassion.
Understanding.

The belief that, in the blackest spots my path reveals,
You will light my way.

∞∞∞

I wouldn't exactly say that I had been estranged from my sister, but the two of us weren't exactly going for brunch regularly either. I love her. She loves me. That never changed. But the frequency with which we saw each other changed dramatically when our living situations evolved about seven or eight years ago.

There was never a time when we couldn't call on each other for help. We just didn't, for the most part. But, when I was in hospital after my stroke, aside from my daughter, who came every single day, there was no one else who was there more than my sister. It didn't surprise me, because despite our recent absence from each other's lives, I know her. I know how deeply she feels things. I know exactly how to drive her insane. I know what matters to her. I do… her little sister.

Each day that she came to see me was a reminder that tragedy can come with blessings, and struggle can come with grace.

My fifteen-year-old daughter visited each day. She would bring me things that I needed and items of comfort. She'd straighten messes in my room, and amidst my communication crisis, having no voice, she would communicate for me when I couldn't. I wouldn't have recovered as thoroughly as I have without her. In truth, I'd have been lost and terrified.

Because of my limited communication with my sister, my

daughter didn't have the chance to establish a meaningful connection with her. But as the three of us sat in my hospital room, sharing concerns and cracking the occasional joke, something started to develop. My daughter found a familiarity and comfort in my sister, and my sister began to see what an awesome young woman my daughter has become. If nothing else had come from two weeks in hospital on oxygen and copious medication, it still would have been worth it.

When I first went to the Emergency Room, my nephew, who lived with me at the time, was with me. Terrified by the assumption that I had just had a stroke, I remember looking at him and pleading "please don't leave me." He reassured me, telling me that he wouldn't, and he settled in for the long haul. In my fear, I didn't consider what a traumatizing place hospitals could be for some people. After many hours in the ER, I could see the effects of the surroundings on his exhausted face. I told him that I would be okay, and I sent him home to sleep. There is no doubt in my mind that, had I not given him leave to go, he'd have remained with me through every step. Though emotionally affected by my lengthy admission process, he came to visit me a few times. That was difficult for him, and I felt loved in his effort to be there for me.

About a year before the stroke, my daughter's best friend moved in with us as well. A girl who chose me as a guardian, who I chose as a beautiful soul worth nurturing. She too made time to visit me and offer comfort in distress.

Upon my return home, my mother stayed at my side and offered the help and comfort that only a mother can.

Among the many blessings I have, and the phenomenal mercy of a strong and fast recovery, I will never fathom what could make me worthy of the people in my life who carried me through that time, and the faith that made me light enough to carry.

In Dedication...

I've never seen compassion bloom, so fully on display,
As my daughter shows, in boundless love, her bold and fearless way.
Of all the blessings I have known, I'll never comprehend,
How I'm worthy of such awesome joy; my sweet and bright godsend.

My sister is of mindful heart,
That sets her spirit worlds apart,
Where she sees others through their pain,
Renewing hope in me again.

My nephew, in God's master plan,
A gentle soul and steadfast man,
Through purity that he inspires,
He'd stand with me and forge through fire.

There is a certain kind of love, that springs solely from a mother.
A faith in you, and hope that thrives, unmatched by any other.

I chose a child, who I love, to join my family.
How blessed I am, she chose me too, and cares so well for me.

The friends who cheered, as fast I rose.
In Jen and Mike, I found repose.
Forever will my spirit know,
Who stood with me amidst the blows.

I'm blessed with family, and with friends,
My God has warmly gifted.
I dedicate this work to them,
By whom I am uplifted.

Thank you for being my greatest blessings.

∞∞∞

I can't imagine the realm of fear that stroke patients must drown in without faith to carry them through. It would be all-consuming. The fear of limitations. The crippling anxiety over the possibility of it happening again. The constant reminder of what is lost.

There are certain statistics that I refuse to look up, knowing that they could overwhelm me in a way that could pull my focus from God's healing. I believe that maintaining faith as a primary path can alter one's life in all the ways necessary to avoid the consequences those statistics would warn me about. So, while I believe in the absolute importance of educating yourself in all of the ways that allow you to take responsibility for your health, and understand the challenges you face, I don't see much utility in spending countless hours reading about my likelihood of depression. Ironically, I think it would be quite depressing.

There are pro-active ways in which I can take responsibility, that I hope will further me along the path of being worthy of God's help in those things that I can't fully control. I can improve my nutrition. If I'm being honest, I really had nowhere to go but up with regard to my diet. I've never been a smoker or a heavy drinker, so I thankfully don't carry the stress of breaking those terribly consuming habits. I can exercise, making my body stronger, and giving my blood motivation to keep pumping. I can eliminate things from my life that cause stress far beyond the benefits they offer. That one's challenging and can mean drastic changes to one's lifestyle. But, if you look at a stroke as the giant "reset" button that it seems to be, it's easier to accept the challenge of what's "new," as an opportunity that God believes you're ready to take on.

God decided the moment I would enter this world. He will decide the moment and method of my departure. I'm hoping for a quick and painless high speed Jet Ski accident at age 129. If faith can move mountains, I think I stand a chance.

A Great Big World

I feared my world would get smaller,
Pushing in from the outside to nestle my perceived limitations.
The fear of being less... knowing less... feeling less, weighing on me.

Surrendering, not to defeat, but to the power of something greater.

Lay your fears at the feet of One who can stomp them out.

Give your breathlessness to the wind itself.

Shake loose from trembling in the arms of an all-encompassing shroud.

In your abandon are worlds upon worlds, and the hopes and possibilities your mind couldn't perceive before the space was made.

A tiny black spot.

With the light of my God, a portal into second chances, new purpose, and a beautiful world you can only see through the depth of tragedy.

∞∞∞

It didn't come naturally to me to set goals as I tried to move forward after my stroke. I had to physically remind myself, more than just once or twice, that life carries on, and that I'm still capable in so many ways. As I continued to prove to myself just how capable I was, others in my life began to recognize as well, and I found comfort when people still sought my skills.

There's an uncertainty that lingers. Not every consequence of a stroke is immediately apparent, and as you progress through the following months, you worry that hurdles may become too large to overcome. You watch the reactions of the people you know, and fear that they'll stop seeing value in what you have to offer. It's a fear brought on by your own insecurity, much more so than by anything they convey.

God's presence in my life, is the fortification of my worth. I was created in perfect nature, by an almighty and wonderful God. I possess unique characteristics that set me apart from every single person. I underwent the trauma of a life-changing event, and I'm still standing. In a world that functions in such perfect flow, God made a place and purpose for me and has kept me here to fulfill it.

When I feel lost, God sees where I am. When I feel empty, His spirit can fill me. I don't need to fear the next step because I'm not alone. But I do need to take that next step and show faith in what I know in my heart to be true. A world of opportunity is at my feet because God has forged my path.

Limits

I used to live life "fancy-free,"
Believing limits weren't for me.
Whatever thought my brain could forge,
I'd march intently straight toward.
A challenge that my body met,
Was fated quest, without regret.

Confined within these limits, new;
My health defining what I do,
I know the questions and the fears,
Eluded for so many years.

Intrepidly, I take a step
And pray it won't lead to regret.
Afraid of what I have to lose,
The cost of quest that I may choose.

I hesitate and gasp for air,
At that which once was laissez-faire.
Living life beyond existence,

Fighting fear with deep resistance,
Finding balance - joy and duty,
Seeking bravery and beauty.
To limit risks, but not potential,
And march toward what's existential.

There's a Stroke Clinic at a hospital that's in a city that's thirty minutes away from me. I didn't know exactly what a Stroke Clinic was, but from the time I was in hospital, I was brought to the understanding that, whatever it was, it was especially important. I needed a referral to the Stroke Clinic. The nurses mentioned it. More than one doctor talked about it. The doctor who released me, who usually came and went from my room like The Flash, lingered long enough to proudly declare he had sent in a referral. When I saw my own doctor a few days after release, one of her first questions was "Have you been referred to the Stroke Clinic?" When I answered "yes," she told me that she'd refer me too, and that I should contact her if they didn't reach out to me within a reasonable amount of time. I came to imagine that the Stroke Clinic was a magical place, where symptoms dissolved, and superheroes in long white coats, with stethoscopes, were developing bionic technologies that would render me impervious to vascular constrictions. Ok... not really. But I was terribly curious.

As it turns out, a Stroke Clinic is a collection of medical specialists who focus all of their attention on strokes. They examine your file to find all the missing tests your other doctors may have overlooked and assess which medications and therapies you require, after examining your file. They know and convey, all the lifestyle changes that you should make in order to prevent another event. They're overflowing with resources and statistics to educate you on risk avoidance. By my best assessment, they're God's unwitting team of soldiers, protecting the precious gift of your future and purpose.

If you have the option of attending a Stroke Clinic, their knowledge offers peace of mind. When we pray, it's not always apparent miracles that appear in response. Sometimes it's resources. Sometimes it tests or challenges, to establish our worthiness, or to make us aware of our own innate capabilities. At the Stroke Clinic, they cheered on my diet changes. They made me feel heroic, in my own way, for reducing my medications for pre-existing conditions. They determined usefulness in the prospect of a two-week test with a Holter monitor and arranged for it to be set up by my local hospital. They wondered at my phenomenal recovery and celebrated with me. I was grateful for the resource of the magical Stroke Clinic realm, and the superheroes who helped to educate me. We populate this world by the billions, to carry each other through. We are here to educate each other and lift one another up. How fortunate I am that God has provided those resources so well.

Resourceful

I am a force of nature; powerful and bold.
Capable beyond my ken, of miracles untold.
A tool of Godly passion, if only I can learn,

What's mine to reach,
What's yours to teach,
My insight must discern.

More than just an instrument, I act in faithful praise,
As my will thrives, engaging right, in whole and selfless ways.

I am not called to rule the world but only play my part.
A role God deems, with faith in me, to be the beating heart.

I am but a resource, harmoniously placed,
To see the Godly spark in you; the role with which you're graced.

∞∞∞

There seem to be a lot of people who view prayer as a wish request service. They think of what they want to achieve and ask God for assistance in doing so. I think I used to look at it similarly. If we're supposed to be mindful of God in all that we do, why wouldn't we request His presence in our efforts to attain our goals? The problem that seemed to present in my own life, was that it called to mind concerns of worthiness. An all-powerful Creator intricately designed me, breathed life into me, sacrificed greatly for my salvation, and I'm going to ask for something more!?! The disbelief in my own audacity, separated me from God. It embarrassed me. It made me question the authenticity of my own faith. It kept me from prayer; from communing with my Creator.

The moment that I realized that I'm not in control, everything changed. What's the point in making endless requests for what you want, when your life's path is determined by what He wants for you?

My prayers are different now. They bring me closer to God. I praise Him for His creation. I thank Him for lifting me out of hell. I trust Him with my life and purpose. He knows what I need. By my gratitude, He knows what I value. In every moment that I remember that, He is gracious, and I am at peace.

I Pray

In awe of Your very creation, I pray.
With gratitude for Your sacrifice, I'm speechless.

How does one find a faith that never waivers?
Through certainty that God can do anything, and that I can do nothing without God?

With knowledge of my mistakes and willful wrongdoings, how can I comprehend the benevolence of the love and compassion that overcomes them?

When I don't trust in Him with all my heart... When I favour my own understanding... I fail.

He is my compass.

He is my Saviour.

How could I be so foolish as to leave my compass behind as I face life's storms?

I pray for strength.

I pray for faithfulness that quells my fears.
I pray to be worthy of the mercy You bestow every day.
I pray to remember that my purpose is to praise You.

May I find the voice to raise in Your honour.
May I find the courage to stand in Your grace
May I know the peace in that surrender.

May I know you closer, Adonai.

I pray

If you've faced a stroke in your own life, I challenge you to find the absolute best parts of yourself following that trauma. I promise you that they are there. Something exists in you that makes you an important part of God's ultimate plan. If you've lost your voice, find meaning in what your soul says. If you've lost your strength, inspire others with your determination. If your mind is confused, within that confusion, poetry exists. A language heard by you and God, that speaks peace. When you feel lost, you can be found. When you are angry at the world for seeing your challenges, and angry at God for putting them in your path, bring it to the table. Lay out all the flaws of a society that recognizes weakness, along with your own, and then show the world how to overcome them!

You can be an inspirational story. You can choose to rise in faith, gloriously, rather than being swatted down as a victim. You just have to be open to believing in something deeper than you believe in yourself. Not because your "self" isn't spectacular, but because your eyes are opened to something greater. There is so much peace in accepting that you aren't in control. There's so much strength in it.

Whole

Inside of you, a poet's voice.
Entangled battles, not by choice.
But rising from a drastic need,
The blessing of a sprouting seed.

Though words inside you may not flow,
The spring that makes the seedling grow,
Faith in God. Belief in you.
You look within to start anew.

You never saw beauty in your face,
Or brilliance in a pensive place,
Til through the blessing of God's grace,
Sprang miracles through faith's embrace.

You are a product of Creation.
The former you, an imitation.
Your life renewed, with purpose measured,
By faith in God, so deeply treasured.

You rise in life to find your role.
You look within, and you are whole.

I like to go for walks. When I look back on my history of fitness efforts, walking is pretty much the whole list. I'm not a cardio junkie or a weight-training type of gal. I've never been into yoga or water aerobics, or tai chi. I walk. If I want to be in better shape, I walk further. When I had a piece of exercise equipment in my home, it was a treadmill... that I could walk on. When I had a gym membership, it was so I could go and use their walking track when there was too much snow outside. Though not an exciting fitness regimen, it's one that has worked for me over the years.

It was just two years ago that I decided to try something new. I saw an ad for a fitness program called "Supernatural." It was a virtual reality exercise program in which you were given the illusion of punching or slashing objects that appeared to be flying in your direction through use of a Virtual Reality headset called an "Oculus." The environments created by the virtual reality could be quite inspirational, as could the music it played as you "boxed" your way to better health. Whether it was the Dolomites, or a beach, or the mouth of a volcano, it inspired a warrior's spirit.

Something has held me back from trying to resume that since my stroke. I looked up the effects of virtual reality on someone who has had a stroke, assuming it might be negative. It turns out that they use it to help with therapy for many patients. I guess the images can kind of trick a mind into believing that it can push beyond its currently perceived capabilities.

My general health has presented new challenges since the stroke. I get tired quickly and deeply. I show physical signs of stress, such as hair loss and lethargy. Perhaps it's just a result of being sedentary for so long with illness, but I have general body ache that causes me to limp for the first few steps each time I get up.

New challenges require new solutions. I'm moved by faith to revisit the Oculus program; that frightens me a bit, because it tricks an already stressed mind. I'm not meant to live in fear of things I knew. I'm meant to thrive in new experiences, and push forward in mastering the things I started in. So, I'm going to do some virtual boxing. I'm going to try the Yoga or the Tai Chi. I'm going to look into swimming. I'm going to do all of that because I'm in God's hands, and there's no safer place to be.

In God's Hands

I needn't fear what I don't know,
For it is but a way to grow.
In faith, I thrive,
My will revived,
Extinguishing intrinsic woe.

I set my cares into God's hands,
Knowing that He has a plan.
I find a peace,
That will not cease.
A reason that I understand.

I know exactly what to do.
Step up. Have faith. Embrace what's new.
Adventure-bound,
On solid ground,
I'm lifted up and carried through.

∞∞∞

I've never believed that the way to bring people to God is unsolicited sermons to their apparently lost souls. While I appreciate the passion of Street Preachers, and the apocalyptic warnings of theologians, I've always thought that the way to guide people to a biblical and spiritual life, is to live it yourself, and to do so spectacularly. You can't preach salvation to others while looking like a rundown mess who needs to be saved. Claiming happiness while living misery, isn't going to win anyone over. Claiming to have faith, while hiding behind excuses, has never made any onlooker declare "Now that's the kind of life I want to live."

Prior to this experience, I never would have had the audacity to try to write a book claiming the benefits of faith. And, while I don't think that the average person is looking at my lifestyle with envy, I feel God's presence in my life. I feel Him restoring me. I feel His direction and support. If Stroke Recovery was an Olympic Event, I'd be absolutely crushing it, and my faith and gratitude would be why.

As my life progresses, I will continue to embrace new experiences and seek out new adventures. But now, I'll do so to see the beauty in God's creation, and the purpose in capability. I'll seek out deeper meaning in the expressions of others, to understand the magic and glory of their purpose in the grand scheme of things. I'll open my heart to find loving connection with people, because the capacity that I've been given for that is endless.

People have flaws. I'll recognize them, learn from them, and hope that others find utility in seeing my imperfections. I will write in verse or song, when the spirit moves me. My voice, once I get it back, will rise in song, with a joy one can only find in God's presence. I will be a testament to faith and recovery and a life well-lived. And if I do it right, someday a doubtful, thirsty soul, will drink in what spills out of me, and they'll find the fulfillment of faith and peace. What a phenomenal day that will be.

Watch and Yearn

Way down deep inside my soul,
A lesson that has made me whole.
If my life is under God's control,
Adventures don't demand a toll.

I could live this life in fear,
Dreading threats within my sphere,
Hiding from a new frontier,
Because my path appears unclear.

Or I could forge ahead, undaunted,
And live in faith, as God has wanted.

To submit in whole to being His,
And truly know what freedom is.

A pain not mine,
A guilt, unearned,
For all is His.
I'm unconcerned.
I spread my wings,
In flight, I've learned
To keep His faith,
So watch and yearn.

I'm a city girl. A small city girl, but one who very much appreciates the modern comforts, and one who dramatically reacts to the presence of an insect, or who whines rather incessantly over high levels of humidity. It makes it rather amusing that my recent connection to my Creator, paired with a fascination for reality tv shows about wilderness survival, is making me want to build a yurt and quest for fire.

It doesn't feel like the solution to my health woes is likely to be found within my air-conditioned walls. I think that, once you feel a call and longing to breathe life in, you have to go to where life thrives. It's funny what that looks like for me in the early stages of recovery. It includes things like wearing many layers of winter clothing, and going for a drive in sub-zero temperatures with the windows down and breathing deeply. It's "baby steps" toward my bug-proof yurt, and my raging, smoke-free fire.

It's not lost on me that we have the comforts that we do because man has spent generations aspiring to ease and comfort. But sometimes, too easy and too comfortable, deprive us of strength and character that can overcome difficult situations that God puts in our path, and accept them with the grace He gave us the capacity to master. Don't live your whole life inside just because it's where the warmth is. God created a beautifully intrinsic world. See it. Learn something from it. Find strength in the ways you can interact with it. And thank God every day that He made you a part of it.

When Nature Calls

The trickle of the water flows, with current pulling under.
A fierce yet peaceful force of life, inspiring of wonder.
The artistry of every leaf that changes for the season.
The tree trunks that are counting years, that sway in wind's cohesion.
The cracking branch and pelting rain; intense and zealous choir,
Fervently resounding with the heat of wildfire.
When it beckons, heed the call. God summons you to "be."
Within your core, it's vast expanse; an unmatched harmony.

You were made with great command, to master all that crawls,
Majestic beasts, and earth's green feast. Submit when nature calls.
You'll heal in spirit, body strong,
When you return, where you belong.

∞∞∞

I watched my hair develop a new silver tint over the first couple of months following my stroke. It was disappointing, but understandable, given the stress my body was enduring. It's not unusual to start to lean toward "arctic blonde" at the age of forty-six. But it was rather shocking how quickly it happened. It was only a month after my stroke when my nephew sat in front of me, looked at me for longer than a glance, and declared with the sound of a breathtaking revelation "You're going grey!" Had that been the whole of it, I feel I might have just accepted it, and started thinking of new ways to embrace my new and deceiving appearance of maturity. But it turns out that hair loss is a side effect to blood thinners, and given how much of it I have to lint roll off of my sofa on a regular basis, I suspect my vanity is in for a challenge. It's either that, or my daughter is successfully hiding a Golden Retriever from me, who she allows to roll on the furniture in my absence, and who's oddly hypoallergenic. Fingers crossed! Show yourself, Rover!

Vanity

When my hair greys, or vastly thins,
When the vision of fatigue begins,
When youthful looks start to decline,

I won't grasp to this face of mine.
For in me, I see new reflection,
The virtue of a clean direction,
And what takes root inside of me,
It leaves no room for vanity.
So shed my hair and crease my face,
A brighter beauty takes its place.
The light of God, its spot demanding,
A deep impassioned understanding.
Departure from a vain obsession,
To embrace in full my life's progression.

I've always enjoyed going for drives with my daughter. We would play loud music and sing our hearts out as we drove. It wasn't just regular singing. It was scream-singing... belting it out like we were Madonna on stage in front of thousands, and our sound equipment had malfunctioned. It was loud and ridiculous and glorious. I still have unresolved vocal cord damage from the cough that accompanied the pneumonia I had at the same time as my stroke. It prevents me from singing, which drives me nuts. I still try to occasionally sing in a reasonable tone, and always end up in noticeable discomfort afterward.

One of the songs that my daughter and I would sing sometimes, was The Big Bang Theory by the Barenaked Ladies. It's a very fast-paced song. It's one of those pieces that isn't terribly impressive in its melody, but if you can manage to get all of those words out, in the right order, it's indicative of a unique talent. Post-stroke, I couldn't. My brain couldn't co-ordinate with my mouth at that pace, and my attempts failed. It was so frustrating. Singing a fast-paced song isn't an important skill to possess. But every time I tried and couldn't do it, I felt like less than what I once was. It was a reminder that my brain was injured, and a part of me was lost.

Over the holiday season, on the first night of Chanukah, I tried singing a song that I sing every year called "Chanukah," which I originally heard sung by an artist named Marty Goetz. It's beautifully spiritual and always feels to me like a musical recommitment to God. This time when I sang it, my voice cracked and cut off; my musical ability drastically diminished. But the connection that I felt ran deeper, and as I started to cry in the middle of the song, I reached for a range I hadn't managed since beginning my recovery, and it came out whole and beautiful for a single sentence. I sang for my God, and He gave me the chops to do it! In that moment of recommitment, I knew that He was with me, and He wanted me to succeed.

If you've never heard their music, you can probably well imagine that a song by The Barenaked Ladies doesn't quite hold the same spiritual message as a song about the miracle of Chanukah. But I was recently reduced to happy tears again, and was knowledgeable of God's blessings, when I once again tried to sing their fast-paced song, and I succeeded. My brain and my mouth co-ordinated. My vocal cords still hurt and my voice still cracked, but I didn't care. Another piece of me was restored, and this time, I was grateful for every syllable that left my mouth.

Raise Your Voice

My voice is Yours; my soul filled with song.
In spirit, I soar, to where I belong,
Within the depths of melodious tune,
And in Your arms, where we commune.

When words in love are meant for You,
There are no limits in what I do,

For perfect in design and cause,
I'm more now than I ever was.

Imperfect to the naked ear,
I pray there's joy in what You hear.
In perfect voice, I raise to You,
Praise and heartfelt gratitude.

Restoring that for which I've longed,
The words and beauty of a song,
The sharpness of a mind, re-lit,
Unrestrained, my heart commits.

∞∞∞

Back in my twenties, as a result of chronic pain, I was prescribed morphine to reduce my levels of discomfort to something tolerable. I took the medication as prescribed, and was grateful for the relief it offered. But over time, I noticed a growing anger taking root inside of me. The fuse that lit my temper grew shorter and shorter the longer I used that medication, and gaining control of it was akin to emotional bull riding. I was trying to tame something outrageously wild. I feel like that history has come into play recently; like I'm calling on skills I haven't needed in a while.

I don't know if it's because of frustration and feelings of restriction. Perhaps it's fed by fear. Maybe it's a chemical change that has developed as a result of what I've experienced. Whatever it is, the bull is showing a little attitude.

Ironically, the answer to the problem of anger, is anger-inducing to me. It's the knowledge that, how I respond to things is a choice. As if making choices feels like a possibility in the midst of the torture of a hot collar. It's one of those instances when I find it very helpful to submit my path to God's hands. When you accept that the outcome is His, and your only responsibility is the choice you make in that moment, the frustration and restriction minimize, and fear goes away, leaving you with just the chemistry to contend with.

You take deep breaths. You try to remove emotion and challenge yourself to evaluate the situation based on logic. You remind yourself of qualities that you've always valued... kindness, understanding and forgiveness. Then, you pray for the grace to overcome in a way that will satisfy the principles that you aspire to share with God.

Sometimes, you'll fail. The bull will toss you clear across the arena. Get back on. Remind yourself of who you want to be. Declare intentions of peace and love, and try again. The only forgiveness you need for your shortcomings, is His, and He's remarkably gracious.

Peace and Love

An irritated mind,
Making me unkind,
A challenge that I find,
Irrationally blind.

Frustration that I feel,
On a level that's unreal.
An ugliness revealed.
A chemistry, unhealed.

Handing up my rage to Thee,
Praying that I may be free,
And find peace and love inside of me.

∞∞∞

I've found that in every stage of my recovery, establishing some sort of routine within my limits, has been key in reaching the next goal. The routine and the goal may have been astonishingly simplistic, but it was always absolutely imperative to success. It started with the goal of staying out of bed for more than two hours at a time. I'd wake up at 9:30 AM each day to try, and would often far surpass my goal. Sometimes I'd fall asleep where I sat. I generally did very little activity, recognizing that I was so very blessed to have help for everyday things like making meals or just a cup of tea. But each day that I surpassed two consecutive hours of remaining conscious, was a day that I accomplished something within my intended time frame.

From there, I aspired to make breakfast for myself. First, it was toast. After a while, I peeled an avocado to go with the toast. When I felt like an absolute champion, I fried an egg! There I was... awake for at least two hours, eating eggs and avocado toast, that I had made.

I had begun my writing exercises while I was still in the hospital. When I got home, I continued as part of my new routine. I wrote something. Some days it was poetry. Some days it was a barely-recognizable signature. Some days it was a typed message to a friend with misspelled words and poor grammar. But I did it every day. I stayed awake for a few hours in a row, ate eggs and avocado toast, and I wrote something.

Every time that I committed to restoring myself in some way, God rewarded me with His blessing, and with a deep appreciation for the things I had so egregiously forgotten to be thankful for. The more I tried to progress, recognizing His gifts and His mercy, the lighter He made my load.

As things stand now, I wake up in the morning and go to bed at night. I can and do write thoughtfully and comprehensively. I cook meals that far exceed the nutritional content of what I used to make. I entertain friends. I go on day-long adventures with family members. I've done a Girl's Night Away with my daughter. In short, I'm living life, happily and openly, with endless simple goals ahead of me to spark the gratitude of every capability God has given to me.

A Simple Step

A simple step; a simple plan,
A simple faith that says "you can."
Progression made, however small,
Restoring gratitude for all.

In simple love, God's grace bestowed;
The blessings you were never owed.

Finding where your first steps lead,
Pushing yourself to achieve,
Knowing that your path is blessed,
Thriving at your God's behest.

Never has a simple thing,
Begot so much of everything,
As you discover second chances,
Enlightened, thoughtful life advances.

You stretch. You grow. You find your depth.
It all starts with a simple step.

∞∞∞

The ultimate goal isn't simply to restore my abilities. It's to use those abilities to further mankind in the recognition and commitment to a faith that enlightens the mind, uplifts the spirit and fulfils an instinctual need. I wonder if aspiring to that is indicative of self-importance. How could I possibly believe that's a purpose God would trust to me? I suppose when I consider that He determines the scale of my success in such endeavours, I can recognize that my words might not reach beyond a single person. But I forge ahead, excited to think that I could make a positive difference in the life of someone else. I might help someone find the words that their mind is too stressed to form. I might leave a struggling person feeling understood. I might inspire someone to find peace in faith.

As I heal from stroke, I sit inside my home, focused on simple tasks and general recovery. But at the same time, I find myself mindful of the need to eventually push outside of these walls and start developing a path to impact the recovery of others. I've started looking into programs like "After Stroke," which is offered by March of Dimes to connect Stroke survivors to others who understand their unique challenges. I've noticed a support group nearby that has physical group therapy and education by guest speakers. I've begun reading about various clinical trials that are being explored by an organization called CanStroke, and I've sought out social media communities of stroke survivors. A whole world of people that I want to help. The comments that I read are overwhelming. Fears that I try to overcome with faith, and defeat and desperation of tortured souls. God, give me the strength to save them. Make me steadfast in my belief, and bright in my example. Every day I am grateful for Your mercy, and every tragic story reminds me how fortunate I am that You spared me the absolute agony of facing this without You.

Meant for More

So much to learn. So far to go.
To push the limits that I know.
Allowing my world view to grow.

Finding what I have to give.
Inspiring through how I live.

God restored so much in me,
I'm meant to give to others;
Put challenges along my path,
And daily, I discover,
The ways we're meant to love, inspire and uplift one another.

May I find passion in the calm,
The poet's wisdom of a Psalm.

May I find purpose, hear the call,
And boldly act, submitting all,
Beyond that which I knew before.
I'm built by God, and meant for more.

My faith faces challenges. I believe that God saved me. I believe that I'm intended for redemption. I know that God's power is absolute. But every time I get a headache, or a pain in my arm, or a heavy feeling, I'm afraid. What used to be "just a headache," or a moderate exhaustion, feels life threatening now.

There's a certain levity in the moments when I remember that

God is in control. The tension that overcomes my body in those moments when I forget, dissolves when I remember. I find irony in the knowledge that the tension I allow myself to feel is likely the greatest actual threat to my health. I aspire to a level of faith that allows me to overcome it with ease.

I recently watched the Disney Live Action movie "Mulan," and there was a statement made in the movie more than once... "There is no courage without fear." It's true. You need adversity for growth. Muscles get bigger by tearing. Fear makes us brave, if we face it with the right mindset. Fear can make us wise if we face it with God. I aspire to wisdom. More than that, I aspire to be worthy of wisdom.

I think that God gave us certain emotions as a test to see if we can overcome them by committing them to Him and submitting to His will rather than our own. How courageous one would have to be to relinquish the illusion of control. May my fear forge that courage, and may I pass every test.

Courageous

The hardest challenge that I face,
The flaw that I cannot erase,
A quality that takes it toll;
My mind will not release control.

I see a world of strength and peace;
A thriving place where all's released.
Joy and beauty made to last,
Are firmly there, within my grasp.

Yet, human nature has its flaws,
And challenges, they have a cause,
I foolishly neglect to see,

That Heaven on earth waits for me.

But someday, I will take that step,
And leave behind worldly regret.
How courageous in my gains,
When I submit to God the reigns.

∞∞∞

I suspect I have a condition which I haven't yet spoken to my doctor about. My preliminary consultation with "Dr. Google" suggests that it's something commonly referred to as "neuropathic itch." It's an itchy scalp brought on by nerve damage rather than a skin condition. I suppose I haven't been anxious to mention it because I haven't come across many solutions to it in my moderate research. Thankfully, it's not constant. But when it flares up, my nails can't get sharp enough or long enough to reach it.

Suddenly, every physical aspect of my life is stroke-related. Problems I've had before that were commonplace, are different and new now. It's a different kind of exhaustion than I've ever had. It's a kind of broken focus that I've previously not experienced. It's an itchy scalp that comes from somewhere deeper, and burns sometimes. When I said I wanted a life filled with new experiences, I likely should have been more specific in my request.

All of these groups and communities of stroke survivors exist because there's a certain understanding and compassion that only comes as a result of experience. If I truly want to help people, I guess the challenges I face have to be impactful enough to teach me how. So far, I accept it as part of God's ultimate plan for me, and I take solace in the belief that He won't give me more than I can handle.

Understanding

If I'm meant to know compassion, understanding and resilience,
I need to grasp potential existing in God's brilliance.
Limitless in finding what a brave soul can endure,
Pursuing depth and clarity, emblazoned, full and pure.

Perceiving and acknowledging the reasons for my fight,
Leaning on my God with faith that He will make it right,
Eyes wide open,
Facing darkness,
That leads me to the light.

Each night, when I go to bed, I take a prescription sleeping pill that reduces anxiety. I never thought there would be a time in my life when I'd need anything for anxiety, but the relief that medication gives me at bedtime is quite strong, and the wave of near panic that I experience in the morning when it wears off, has me actively seeking the proper nutrition to reduce it. There's a supplement that I take called Mag Malate Renew from AOR. It's magical. It noticeably reduces my pain and, if I've forgotten to take it the night before, the morning anxiety wave definitely reminds me. I try to eat the right foods; snacking on bananas and pistachios and pumpkin seeds, opting for avocado toast for breakfast and choosing decaffeinated beverages. It makes a difference.

God gave me the tools to help myself, and I feel like I'm making good choices as I strive for progress and inner peace. I don't feel insufficient for requiring medical intervention in situations where I've made every effort to utilize God's pharmacy first. But I need to know that I've tried to help myself before employing the help of others. I feel like it's an important part of faith to draw from what God has made you; to summon your strengths and grow your knowledge. When you've done that, and find that you just don't have the answers, I believe that's the reason we all share the experience of life together. What each of us can see and do are compliments to build each other up. When I count my blessings, I count my abilities first. They're the tools with which I can further those I love, and those who feel suppressed.

Blessings

You blessed me with the written word,
And inspired me to write it,
Infused me as an advocate,
With a cause and will to fight it.
I have in me a planner's mind,
Detailed to perfection,
Logic and inspired thought,
Prone to introspection.

You gave me wit, enough to charm,
And sometimes coax a smile.
My will is geared to honesty,
You teach me kinder style.

Of all the blessings I could name,
None are counted quite the same,
As the purpose You've allowed to me,
To contribute to my family.
And as I grow in faith and love,
To see Your mercies rise above,

The next stage in my life-long story,
Is to use my blessings to Your glory.

∞∞∞

Helen Keller once said "I cried because I had no shoes, until I met a man who had no feet." I think of that quote a lot as I read the testimonies of other stroke survivors. For some, what they write is an expression of the depths of their suffering. For others, it's a bold testament of strength and perseverance. I've had days when I've felt utterly defeated by the least of my symptoms. There's a feeling of guilt that follows complaining about my itchy scalp or frequent need for a restroom, when there are others paralyzed, unable to swallow, or form a sentence.

How do you help people who are carrying the weight of the world on their shoulders, when you feel crushed by the weight of fatigue or a headache? Jesus brought Lazarus back to life. He told a paralyzed man to get up and walk, and he did. The power of God is absolute. The power of me, is determined by God.

Be it through faith or positive attitude, I see some people who are peaceful warriors. They fight unimaginable adversity day after day, and rise with a fierce smile every morning. What gives them the ability to do that? Why them? Perhaps I'm not meant to know every reason. But I watch, with interest; with fascination, as God imbues some with the phenomenal ability to inspire others... to inspire me.

Whatever you struggle with, is unique to you, and the way that you cope is contingent on so many aspects of who you are and the strengths and abilities that you possess. Someone else's mountain is your mole hill, and vice versa. I've noticed the incredible strength of the human spirit since my stroke. As each of us "rewires" and tries to accept the differences we see in ourselves, I see so many finding a steady foundation in themselves by the action of lifting others up. When so much is stripped away, we seem to find a deeper gratitude for what remains, as well as finding a desire and responsibility to help others find it. I didn't have that purpose or perspective before, and I recognize it as an incredible gift.

Samson

I once saw a tiny chipmunk, who passed by me every day,
Lift a tomato twice his size to carry it away.
I sat and watched his mighty feat in awe and fascination,
As he defied all logic, when spurred by inspiration.

How could such a little thing find strength beyond his size?
Was it need, or promise of a great rewarding prize?
What arose inside of him that made him know he could?
Was it limitless perception, or faith that said he should?

He showed me the potential in the tiniest of things;
A fortitude beyond the norm that need and passion brings.
I named him Samson for his strength; the mightiest of creatures,
As joyfully revealed to me, my fuzzy little teacher.

I've seen it in so many since that shocking great display;
The burden that would overwhelm, somehow we find a way.
Collapsing columns of the walls that seek to keep us in,
Finding that, at our rope's end, another length begins.

Sometimes it's just "one of those days." Oh, how I struggle to not have too many of them. The days when you feel nothing but self pity, and an underlying tone of guilt for not being sufficiently grateful for what you have.

By all accounts, I've had a pretty spectacular life. I've travelled to incredible places and had unique experiences. I haven't just met some of my heroes. I've travelled with them, worked with them to help others, and had meaningful interactions with them. I've ridden an elephant bareback into a river. I've raced on Seadoos around Lady Liberty. I have been a single mother to the world's greatest child, and have seen art and adventure in ten thousand things with her. I've had breakfast at Tiffany's and dinner in world famous restaurants. I've parasailed off of a beach and landed in shark-infested waters. I've ziplined in Honduras and laid down with tigers in Thailand. I've stood in awe of timeless art and incredible architecture in Italy. I got lost in the south of France. I've published a book. I've both spoken and sang to sizeable audiences. I've planned wildly successful events to the benefit of charitable organizations. Should I not be fully satisfied? The ability to accomplish each one of those things was a gift, for which I could never claim to be deserving. Now, I wake up each morning with knowledge of how fragile life is, and I hunger for adventure, while still feeling as though I lack worthiness.

I'm endlessly grateful that I can stand and put one foot in front of the other. I'm deeply thankful for my ability to make breakfast for my child and me, and to sit and talk with her each day and to go out for coffee together sometimes. Each breath is a blessing, and I'm so frustrated by the part of me that yearns to ride the elephant or battle the sharks, because it feels so terribly selfish and so desperately far away from where I am now.

I've tried to sort out why it's so important to me to live a life so big and full of adventure; and the ways that the importance of that has changed recently. I think that what was once actions I took to establish relevance, has become challenges I face to determine competence. And I think that's so important to me because there has never been a more terrifying time in my life to not be anyone's first priority.

Stripped to my most basics parts, when I look around at what's missing, in the absence of all else, God remains. I imagine He wants me to soak in art and ride a Seadoo or two. More than that, I imagine He wants me to find satisfaction in the choices and effort I make in my day-to-day life to make me feel worthy. So, I will aspire to do that. If I only have two good hours in a day, I will actively start thinking of ways that I might use them to help others. There is some moment of each day when I could feed a hungry person, or help someone with health more challenging than mine. The challenge is in finding those opportunities, but God didn't take the time to re-wire me for nothing. The path is in there. Perhaps finding it is the adventure I'm missing.

Never Enough

The hunger of a thousand men, a thirst that goes unquenched,
A selfish longing deep inside, thriving and entrenched,
A need I feel to see and do what I've never done before,
And once I've seen and done it all, I want to seek out more.
A new place or adventure that makes me feel alive,
The metaphoric summit, for which my spirit strives.

To what end do I seek it out?
What is this hunger all about?

I've never seen this world in ways that others clearly do.
The knowledge of a million scholars, in my world, is untrue.
Inside out and upside down; life from my perspective;
A world that's on a different plain, passionately reflective.
How can I live inside a box where nothing reflects me?

And how can I be satisfied in ways others seem to be?
I seek out what is different and reach for unreal things,
Knowing that my truth could shine in what exploration brings.

Perhaps God speaks to me through passion, desire and unrest,
And I will find my peace in worlds revealed at His behest.

When comes the time that I can see,
The view that He entrusts to me;
A vision only I can know,
My backward sight could only show.

I will find my purpose, in the new truth that I see;
That passion for a lively world, instilled inside of me,
And now with deeper meaning and compassion for divergence,
With hope and hunger to define a spiritual resurgence,
I'll help the disenfranchised know,
The means to cause their world to grow.

With minds reset and hearts that long,
Unique souls will arise in song,
And find a place where they belong.

There are no words to describe the depth of stubbornness in human nature. We demand to see signs of God and outright miracles as proof of His presence and power, and then we refuse to see them when they're right in front of us. My brain went a time with no oxygen, and I'm still here. I'm writing and speaking and drawing breath. Make no mistake. If you have survived a stroke, you are a miracle. If you have regained abilities that you had initially lost, you are blessed.

I've always known that God exists. It has long baffled me that people search to explain the brilliance, beauty and intricacy of nature's balance with stories of cosmic dust rather than divinity. To believe in the divine means that you accept the understanding that something greater than you exists. It's phenomenal how many people are terrified by that thought. I suppose it boils down to accountability. I don't think many people start out life with aspirations to become "the bad guy." But, there's a certain comfort in believing that you're at the top of the food chain when you fear falling short of perfection.

To me, it's absurd to look at the rings of a tree trunk that count its years, or the purity of water filtered through stone… or the face of my daughter, and to try to attribute any of it to anything less than an all-powerful Creator. Admittedly, I've met a few people who are solid cases for the theory of man's descendants from apes, but I was fearfully and wonderfully made by God. My brain is creating new pathways to allow me to live and thrive. I am the paralyzed man who took up his bed and walked. I am the blind man who can now see. I am the leper cleansed of illness. A world of people don't see what I know to be true. For some reason, I am blessed. And with this knowledge, I absolutely fear falling short of perfection, which I believe is a blessing in itself. May I rise every day with the motivation to live soulfully and purposefully, and to move closer to God's glory than where I was yesterday.

Miracle

What defines a miracle? You do. The breath that infuses life into your body and soul, the unique passions that set your mind on fire and the delicate balance of effort and ease; strengths and weaknesses, that make you fully whole.

What almost slipped away, raises you up and beats you down in unison.

You are a builder, an educator and a powerful force of reckoning within yourself, empowered by divine agency.

What defines a miracle? The beauty and intricacy of a mind that finds a path at the behest of passion, effort and faith.

You find a word. You lift a finger. You take a step.

What defines a miracle? The Creator does, through blessing and grace.

Following my stroke, I was put on a medication for cholesterol. My levels were well within normal range, but I was told that normal range isn't the goal for a stroke patient. My doctor wanted the number lower than average. It made sense to me to reduce cholesterol as much as possible because, as I understand it, that widens the passageway for blood to flow. So, I was prescribed the lowest dosage of Rosuvastatin (Crestor,) and I willingly took it. A couple of days ago, upon receiving the results of bloodwork to check my cholesterol levels, a doctor informed me that my liver numbers were quite high. It was just a few years ago that my dad died from liver failure. My nephew, with whom I'm very close, was admitted to Sick Kids hospital with liver failure when he was very young. I've spent the past couple of days worrying, focusing on my family history, and forgetting to exercise faith. Through my own assessment, I've established what's new in my life that might contribute to liver issues; the Crestor and a sleeping pill, both of which can cause liver enzymes to spike. I've consulted with a doctor who advised me that I could stop the Crestor for now, and we'd re-test my cholesterol in a month.

When I was in the hospital, despite my asking the nurse to check twice, there was one night when she failed to find the order for my sleeping pill. With terrible body ache, aspirated pneumonia and the anxiety of being in isolation after a stroke, I remember that as one of the worst nights I have experienced. With memories of that lingering, I'm genuinely afraid to try to wean off of the sleeping pill, but I feel like it's the right thing to do. God gave us our senses for a reason. Our bodies talk to us in both subtle and not-so-subtle ways. It's time to try to lose a crutch. It's time to pray.

As a woman of faith, I know the solution to my barrage of problems. But there's something about human nature that beckons me to wallow in the depths for a while before submitting my trauma to God. My poor brain. My poor liver. My poor vocal cords. Woe is me.

Despite offering me wings to give me flight in spirit and endeavour, I still fall sometimes. I lose my way until the light calls me back. Faith isn't easy. I feel like it should be, but it's not. How thankful I am that God has patience and grace. With Him, I will find restoration a million times, and then a million times more, because that's how He made me.

Fallen

Fallen angels, broken wings,
A silenced choir tries to sing,
A shattered spirit claws at sand,
A drowning man who needs a hand.

Desperately, a soul cries out,
In panicked thirst, amidst the draught,
Crippled by a dark distraction,
Imprisoned by my own inaction.

My faith ensnared in baseless doubt,

Forgetting what my call's about.

It's fear that brought me to this place,
And gave the outside demons space.
It made me question, whole and true,
What God has built me up to do.

But there is not a single thing,
That faith in Him could fail to bring,
And He didn't build and raise me up,
To watch me spill out from my cup.

So I remember who I am, and what my purpose is,
I'll rise in faith and mend my wings, remembering I'm His.

∞∞∞

I do more now than I did pre-stroke. Because I've always had health problems, regular activity has always been a challenge for me, and fatigue has always been an issue. It wasn't the same issue it is now. Post-stroke fatigue is a new level of crippling. My brain feels heavy and my body struggles to read its signals to move. But, whether it's the challenge of proving myself capable after a traumatic event, or the motivation to use the skills that I had temporarily lost, I make a greater effort. I keep my home cleaner. I prioritize breakfast with my daughter, even if I don't have the strength to make it until afternoon. I don't start writing and then forget about it for days. It's important to capture the thoughts that God uses to motivate me. They might motivate and inspire others. I do more, knowing that what I do matters.

A second chance affords you the opportunity to face everything with the wisdom you gained from your first try. You make adjustments to your failures. You prioritize based on the things that you recognize have deeper meaning and forget about the things the world told you ought to have the most meaning. You assess the path to happiness as finding and following purpose. I don't claim to be enlightened by the action of stroke, but my life and priorities have changed, and some things that once mattered to me, seem silly now, and every action I take, is an accomplishment and a gift.

I'm learning that, when my body can't push forward, it's time to exercise my brain instead. When my thoughts are too foggy to make progress, it's time to grow my faith. "Self care" means working myself to the bone to achieve the physical, mental and spiritual depths that make me worthy of the life I have, and living fully in the gratitude that I have this life. I'm "under renovation," with the grand opening coming. Stay tuned because I'm working hard.

Second Chances

The value of a second chance cannot be fully measured,
And the gift of mercy it bestows, make vast and deeply treasured.
It bears with it a duty, to both yourself and others,
To find a path of purpose that elevates another.

Focused on the wisdom that you gained from that first try,
You become the missing piece that made your effort go awry.
Learn with open heart and mind, while pushing through your fear,
The reason and the purpose for which God has kept you here.
Embrace the hope of better times; that great rewarding hour,
Tap into the faith of God, that gave you endless power.

A second chance is both a gift and responsibility;
A charge bestowed in higher love from life's One Deity.

Make worthy of yourself the chance to grow to something more.
Commit in spirit all that makes you greater than before,
And watch as God enables you to spread your wings and soar.

∞∞∞

I've never feared getting sick so much in my life. How will I cope with sinus problems when it's a challenge to swallow? What will a sore throat or cough do to my already inflamed vocal cords? When fever gives me a terrible headache, how will my newly anxious mind react?

The last time I was sick, ended in a stroke. My mind correlates those things now, and I have a school-aged child who hikes off to that giant Petrie dish every morning, tempting fate with teens who are far less health conscious than she is.

If I couldn't submit that fear to God on some level, I think I might go insane. But I don't believe that He has restored me from stroke just to take me out with a cold, and the stress of contemplation will only push my immunity down. So, I'm learning to push through the fear.

What If?

Worried. Panicked. Terrified.
A doubt that's brewing deep inside,
Retreating to the place I hide,
With woes that I cannot abide.

What if my monsters track me down?

What if peace just can't be found?
What if my number comes around?

Unwilling to accept of this,
That life is merely to exist.

But every threat, it scares me more,
And shakes my faith right to its core.
It challenges, unlike before,
To lean on God a little more.

The reward; a promise mercy's giving;
To once again know joy in living.

Carefree as I render all,
The fears and woes that made me fall.

Fiercely, I will rise in light,
My centre strong, my future, bright
And fearless on the path that's right.

∞∞∞

Every time I feel overwhelmed by stress or anxiety, I remind myself of the stark lesson... Life can change in an instant, and what I believe to understand as my likely future, may not be the future that God intends. There are ebbs and flows in our lives that make it a frightening notion at times to not be in control, and a great comfort at other times.

I used to have an idealistic idea of how life would go. I'd always be entirely capable and open to adventure. In my mind, somehow inflation would never happen, but my income would miraculously grow by leaps and bounds. My home was secure. My bucket list was prioritized so that I wouldn't miss anything.

No one in my life would ever suffer, because only those distant from me are subject to trauma. Do you know the problem with idealism? It doesn't do a thing for your character, and it doesn't further the prospects of anyone.

I define success differently now. My ideal is no longer a prioritized bucket list of adventures. I aspire to change a life by inspiring a meaningful lifestyle. I want to grow someone's faith, and I know I can only do so by fully embracing my own. One day, I will create an adventure for someone convinced that his or her life won't allow it. My mind will innovate new joys and abilities for those who feel crippled by both. Perhaps someday I will still jet ski in Fiji and summit Sinai to talk to God. But, when I manage to do the former, the latter will just be icing on the cake.

I saw a photo of a page in a book. The entire content of that page was "Maybe your path is harder because your calling is higher." That's the outlook that motivates me. I'm on this path for a reason. I haven't just put my faith in God. God put His faith in me. It took a stroke for personal growth of depth and meaning. A difficult path, for sure. But, I can be taught.

Eyes Wide Open

Feeling through a rosy haze,
Of wild life and crooked doors,
Accepting undefining ways,
And paths you know deep down, aren't yours.

You grasp at joys and beg for bliss,
For moments that inflate your story;
Adventures that you couldn't miss,
In settings that define your glory.

You grope to find, in darkened rooms,

With eyes closed tight to brighter ways,
Masked purpose that your mind assumes,
Will fill your soul and bring you praise.

Then, in an instant, you descend,
And scales fall from your eyes.
The fog on which your view depends,
Wafts up into the skies.

The brighter path from which you've hidden,
Shines too bright to ignore.
A depth of knowledge, once forbidden,
Enlightens deep within your core.

You dare not close your eyes,
Or attempt to look away,
For what you see is wise.
For what you learn, you pray.

And though you tremble at the thought,
Of worlds unknown and minds impressed,
Your eyes wide open, purpose sought,
Your life finds meaning, wholly blessed.

The way that my head feels post-stroke, is almost indescribable. A headache is more than a headache now. My vision becomes unfocused. I exhaust from mere moments of it. There's a feeling of pressure that I'd describe more as fullness or tightness than a contributor to the pain. It's fragmented. It feels like ache interrupted by breaks in the cohesive thought that allows me to comprehend a new feeling. At times, I think it's amplified by a fear of what it might be, that makes every fibre of my being tense.

I often wonder how long it will take that tension to abate long-term. I feel certain that God will lead me to a place where I no longer live in fear and anticipation of another event, but I think it might serve a purpose right now. A stark reminder that now probably is not the time to try skydiving or deep-sea diving. Now is the time to carefully heal, so that someday, adventures can resume.

I'm not used to fearful living. I've always been a "throw caution to the wind" type of gal, and it has served me well for the most part. It wasn't a part of my personality that I ever sought to change, but I'm learning the difference between "carefree" and "faithful."

Living with faith can unburden you in a meaningful way, while living carefree requires a certain amount of willful ignorance. I choose faith. I choose the knowledge that, with patience and commitment to my own recovery, I will someday learn to live more comfortably with the new expressions of pain and discomfort that my body has developed, and find joy and adventure within the ever-expanding world that my faith and effort creates.

Afraid

If I never rise, I'll never fall,
Safe within these pristine walls,
I take no risk in living free,
Lest death might take a swing at me.

A prison of my own design,
In comfort fashioned in my mind,
To give illusion of a cause,
And never long for all that was.

But I have seen the world outside,

And know my spirit can't abide,
Endurance of my fear's persistence,
To live a life of mere existence.

There are certain fears I'm meant to know,
To reign me in and make me grow,
And certain things I'm meant to face,
That call me to escape this place.

Once in darkness, bathed in light,
A ray of hope, exuding bright,
The key to all I seek outside,
In God, my faith and woes confide.

∞∞∞

With a new threat in my life of spiking liver enzymes, and my deeply felt connection to the Creator, I find myself feeling a deep desire to "go natural" in my health journey.

My diet used to be atrocious. If it wasn't deep fried or chocolate-covered, it held little appeal to me. I liked sugary, creamy drinks and desserts of all kinds. Since my stroke, by God's great mercy, I haven't wanted to those things. For months, I've craved eggs and avocados, whole wheat toast, bananas and pistachios. I want to drink water and tea. I can still have the occasional slice of tiramisu with some berries, but when I try to eat a chocolate bar or fast food, I feel like absolute garbage. Just last week, I found myself eating celery and cucumber to get the taste and feeling of peanut butter cups out of my mouth. I find myself looking up which foods might help the problems that I have. Many of the things I crave meet that description.

Seeing my liver enzymes spike recently, I assessed the new

medications that might have caused that, and I've aspired to come off of as many as safely possible. The most difficult to wean off of has been the sleeping pill. Just as I was reaching the end of that battle, I went to an appointment with an Ear, Nose and Throat Specialist to assess my vocal cord damage, and he wrote me a new prescription. I filled it, but every bit of me has been screaming out to not take it. I'm awaiting liver ultrasound. My bloodwork has shown poor results twice. I don't think I should take it.

Immediately after filling the prescription, I found myself at the health food store, buying all of the things suggested to alleviate my newly diagnosed problem. I saw a poster once that was labelled "God's Pharmacy." It was a deeply fascinating visual of how the foods we eat are often shaped like the organs they benefit most. Walnuts help the brain. Red grapes, in their convenient clusters, help the blood. Citrus fruits look like mammary glands and help lymph movement and breast health. A tomato, with its four chambers, is good for the heart. Don't get me wrong. I see great value in allopathic medicine, and I recognize the medications that I should most likely continue. But, not every drug is a life saving vessel to hop onto, and I find myself wanting to defer to what God has offered first.

Of Nature

Perfect in its balance.

The intricacy of creation; beautiful in its structure; purposeful in every fragment.

The circle of life... of nature... that completes a question and answers it at the same time.

Fruits that sweetly feed my passion.
Greens and whites that build my body.

Poison challenges my soul.

The battles of weakness, make me strong.
Inquisition of purpose, makes me wise.
Questioning the value of my abundance, makes me well.

The key to life, fashioned by God, of nature.

The world that He gave to me, can heal me.
Every living thing supports me, through the divinity of a lesson, the curiosity of my nature, the beauty of what's fresh and clean, and the rock solid ground on which I confidently plant my feet.

The earth. My inheritance. Hiding health and happiness in its veins, as my Creator strips away its secrets one by one.

What is of nature, sustains me.
What is of spirit, binds me to what creation lays at my feet.

I give thanks for my abundance.

Throughout my life, I've been largely misunderstood by people. I've always thought a little differently, acted a little strangely, and felt generally out of sync with this world. As a forty-six-year-old woman, that doesn't really bother me. I'm comfortable within my reality, even when others aren't there with me. But, as a child and a teen, I found it quite difficult. I wasn't confident or interesting to people then. I was just weird. And every way that I tried to express myself, came out wrong... except when I wrote in free verse. As a writer, words that I didn't realize I knew, flowed from my fingertips like the paintbrush of an artist, with a thousand distinct colours. I'd read my creation and understand thoughts and feelings within myself that were unclear before. It was a language that my peers didn't speak, expressing thoughts that they never shared. I knew that it was beautiful because it didn't require the approval of anyone. It was a piece of me, impervious to the edits of poor grammar or unclear language, because it was pristine in intent and presentation.

When I had my stroke and lost my language, I lost a huge and important part of myself. I lost the therapy of writing my way to understanding. I lost the code with which I could occasionally cross my world with the world of others. I lost one of the most valuable skills that God had ever given to me. I couldn't speak or write the sentiment that overwhelmed me. I couldn't even clearly form a statement within my mind. A brew of confusion filled my head, and I had no way to expel it.

Until the end of time, I will never lose gratitude for my restored ability to write. With every word I put to paper, I carry the hope that I might inspire one person. I might help one soul feel more understood. I might spark faith. With every sentence that flows, the therapeutic value knows no bounds, and I heal a little more. I pray that God will guide my thoughts and my pen, and I'm certain that He does, as my words seem right, my intent feels pure, and my sentiment leans into Him. In this way, I am more than I was before. Blessed are You, eternal my God, who rebuilds me with purpose and prose.

Words

Words spill forth and fill my page,
With introspection, love and rage.
Expressions I feel running free,
Released from every part of me.

The beauty in a single phrase,
Sustains my core, my mind ablaze,

Preserving truth that's fully mine,
As art and language intertwine.

Capturing a piece of me,
For all the world to boldly see,
As bright it shines in Godly colour,
Distinctly novel; like no other.

Words that are my very own,
That reach outside; I'm not alone.
Protected pieces of myself,
Impervious to harm itself.

The power of a thought well blessed,
The peace to put your mind at rest,
To spark a passion, raise a query,
Or offer hope to one who's weary.

Cherished as my greatest gift,
I praise You, God, for all of this.

∞∞∞

Faith needs to be fed. It's why we pray ritually. It's why many have a weekly service at church to attend. It's why bibles are in nightstands at hotels. Our connection to God has to be renewed every day. Those of the Jewish faith adhere to six hundred and thirteen rules to remind them of the presence of the Creator in their lives. Every day demands a new commitment. That's how fickle we are. I'm not suggesting that after a day of missed prayer you'll be looting villages and hanging out in shady places, doing unspeakable things, but the further we stray from our engagement with God, the easier it is for our souls to depart from a righteous path.

I look for things to feed my spirit. A gospel song or two… a prayer app on my phone… lectures or articles from others finding faith. I began watching the television show “The Chosen” out of curiosity over its success. I continued watching it because it began to feel like the most successful ministry I’ve ever witnessed. It depicts Jesus and His apostles as rich and meaningful, real people. It tells stories in ways I can imagine them happening. It reminds me that God doesn’t seek out the perfect. He brings in the sheep who goes astray. It inspires a connection to God that I’m quite thankful to feel, as I watch Matthew as a careful writer of Jesus’ lessons, and Peter as the imperfect man who was blessed with deeper purpose.

Those stories anchor me. My mistakes are human, and what I aspire to is Godly. Connecting with the faith of others reminds me that we all face challenges, but those who honour their blessings can find their way back to righteousness. It isn’t just in church that the righteous congregate. Nor is it solely the adherents to organized religion who find connection and lift each other’s spirits. May God lead me to my community and give me the wisdom to embrace it.

Bring Me In

Inspire me to service.
Call on me to prayer.
Ignite my hopeful spirit,
To faithful, loving care.
Open me to see it all;
Blessings everywhere.

A moving song,
A thoughtful story,
A deep, inspired

Call to glory.
A mission steeped,
In blissful meaning,
With Godly purpose,
Intervening.

Plunged into a flowing stream,
Baptized in His deep esteem,
Breathing in, my soul redeemed,
As Chosen stories brightly beamed,
In praiseful peace to fevered dreams.

Bring me in,
To inspiration.
Abiding, pithy
Revelation.
Wrap me in it
Evermore,
Consuming
To my very core.

Hold me tight
And don't let go.
For this is all
I hoped to know,
That all encompassed,
In my mind,
Devotion that's
Uniquely mine,
Of depth and grace
You'll rarely find.

Refresh my hope.
Revive my light.
Remind me
Of the way that's right.
I cling to You,

My God, I pray,
Bring me in
When I'm astray.

∞∞∞

I know that my faith is real and deep because I don't awaken in absolute panic every day. With the health problems that limit my ability to work, my current trajectory has me on course to have a total monthly income of just over half of the average cost of rent on a one-bedroom apartment. In twenty-six months, without the charity of family, I will be homeless. A prospect made more stressful by the knowledge that the family I count on for such charity, is on a trajectory to lose the ability to help. Without divine intervention, my future seems bleak. But it's not. Whatever I face, I'll face it with God. Whatever I feel, whether it's the fullness of His mercy, or the humility of a cardboard box and a blanket, I'm called to recognize its value.

I wonder what will happen, but I don't fear it the way that I once would have. I'm not fearless, but the concern that I have stems from the probability that what I face will be difficult. No one looks forward to hard times. But it's not the easy path that builds phenomenal people. Character and wisdom are forged in uncomfortable circumstances.

Creating discomfort for me isn't really difficult to do. When I get out of bed in the morning, I can barely manage a step without my luxurious, supportive slippers. If I don't start my day with my avocado toast, eggs and tea, my body doesn't feel right. I sleep on a special mattress pad at night that's meant to reduce pain. I've spent years of poor health cracking the code of which costly supplements actually feed my body what it needs to work properly. My ability to function at my current level, is tenuous at best, and discomfort seems inevitable.

Fearful, yet optimistic, I look for opportunities to my use skills that may result in relief, while accepting that God is in control. I will put my best foot forward into something meaningful, and hope that He causes the new ground I set foot on, to flourish.

On Solid Ground

When I was hurt, I found compassion for those in pain.

When I was lost, I began to see fear in the eyes of others.

A bleak future opened my eyes to a spectrum of light dependent on God's mercy.

If tomorrow I'm without a home, or food to nourish me,
I'll find within my poet's sphere, a new soliloquy,
That bolsters through the hope and faith of personal reflection,
The chance to be a better me, with passionate direction.

If plunged with others to the depths of worry and despair,
I will not bask in sullenness, for God will meet me there.
He'll give me strength and spark my mind, to cultivate solutions,
To raise myself and others to our next great evolution.

When I feel overwhelmed by stress and I'm lacking understanding,
I'll raise my voice in desperate prayer, my fighter's soul commanding.
In love I will find comfort. In God, I'll find my home.
In purpose, I'll find nourishment, clothed in prayerful tone.

The stones that life can cast at me, will never see me break,
But raise me up as I build steps no timid soul could take.

∞∞∞

Sometimes I feel like a failure at everything. I can't function well enough to get my dishes done because I couldn't manage more than an hour of sleep the night before. I have family members who feel unloved or abandoned because I keep to myself to cope with my new life challenges and try to accomplish things on my own to find a feeling of capability. My child is devastated by changes I can't control. People inquire about my health and then get frustrated when I talk about the effects of my stroke. I spend time looking at job descriptions, trying to call on my inner warrior to find the strength to take one on, and I pass out halfway through reading the list of qualifications. I fantasize about education to better myself, then find myself re-watching a twenty-minute television program because I lost focus ten minutes into it. Though I feel as though I have much to contribute emotionally and intellectually, I feel like an absolute drain on those I love.

I recognize and mourn every one of those feelings, embracing the reality of them with the acceptance that I'm trying my best to cope and achieve reasonable expectations. Among the many challenges God has placed on my path, guilt and feelings of insufficiency are among the toughest demons I face. There's something about knowing that the Creator took the time to recreate me that emboldens me in the pursuit of overcoming. Whatever shortcomings I may have; whatever ball I've dropped... I was worth a second chance. On the grand scale, I'm a net positive, and in those times when I don't see it, my God does. With the knowledge that part of my value exists in my ongoing focus of being more and doing more, I commit to the unspoken contract to try to be a lighter soul to carry for as long as He holds on to me.

Worthy

Though I falter on my way,
Of facing demons every day,
Above the scream of near defeat,
When courage is in full retreat,
I doubt, but know inherently,
Amidst my flaws, that hope chose me.

I find among the prickly thorns,
Of inside fear and outside scorn,
A nature marred by imperfection;
A spirit searching for direction.
Comfort grasps, endearingly,
With purpose that I know chose me.

Collapsing health in winter's glare,
A season drowned in deep despair,
Calling me to just give in,
And let the weight of sickness win.
Upright, I stand, defiantly.
I choose life and life chose me.

And when I feel that I'm not strong,
And worry that I can't go on;
Am I worthy? Can I grow?
Seeking answers that I know,
For this, embracing openly,
I cannot fail, for God chose me.

Have you ever noticed that you go through life not worrying about any potential health problems or predispositions, then suddenly, you have to worry about all of them? It's not gradual. One day, you're filling out a family medical history on a spa intake form, and the next you're getting tested for everything Mom, Dad, your grandparents and your closest aunts and uncles ever darkened the door of an Emergency Room for.

I hadn't really stopped to think about it much before my stroke. It was just a few years ago that my dad died of liver failure. My grandparents had heart problems. There have been numerous cases of cancer in my family. In the last few months, I've had a scope to check for potential cancerous threats in my vocal cords, bloodwork that showed spiking liver enzymes, two-week long heart testing, brain scans, CT scans of heart and brain, ultrasounds of throat and liver, and assessment of my optic nerve. Prior to all of that, I honestly can't recall how long it had been since I had seen a doctor.

A year ago, I was indestructible. Since then, I've grown a little in wisdom and responsibility. God charged me with the physical, emotional and spiritual repair of this incredible machine that can repair and re-wire itself into something new or different. I'm not going to hand it over to natural decay. It's time for a few upgrades and a general maintenance program. A diet and activity that sustains my body, initiatives that challenge my mind and prayer that feeds my soul.

It's difficult living in a place that's under snow for so much of the year. I crave to move in sunshine... to grow things... to be moved by waves and grounded by dirt beneath my feet. I struggle with the motivation to exercise my body absent of those things. But I eat what fuels me after researching what those things are. It's hard to imagine what will capture my mind and move me forward amidst exhaustion that destroys my focus, but I continue to write when I can, and read about things that interest me. My first priority is to align my faith to strengthen me to overcome those challenges. My body is not invincible, but my spirit is.

Unbreakable

Cast in titanium; a spirit that repels doubt in the stance of a warrior.
My body breaks, but my back stands upright at the behest of a soul that refuses to rest.

Test me. I am ready.
Question my faith. I have answers.

God built this temple, not of flesh and bone, but of love, charity and empathy that endures forever.
My purpose, subject to His care.
My shell, blessed by His mercy.
What belongs to the Creator is indomitable.

I submit my will to beauty and wonder and endless promise;
The inheritance of faith.
The value of a breath is wholly this… to sustain the vessel of what stones and arrows cannot touch.

In one of the social media groups I follow, I saw someone postulate about the possible virtues of a community formed solely of stroke survivors. It struck me as smart and tragic and warm and desperate. I'm not unfamiliar with the challenges of feeling misunderstood. You never fully accept a feeling of being out of sync with the rest of the world. There's nothing that can force understanding in others; no action that fully conveys a message of who you are and what you need.

There are no words with which I can accurately describe the feeling of post-stroke fatigue. But I can tell you exactly what it looks like. It looks like laziness. It looks like someone just isn't trying hard enough. It looks like depression. It is none of those things.

I want to be able to explain to you why that person you've known and loved is so different than they once were… turning introverted and changing priorities that once defined them. It wasn't a choice. It was a looking glass they fell through, that carried them into a new world where they can't survive by the same means that once served them.

When you learn things from infancy, they're innate. Your brain develops its natural path to understanding, coping and reacting. When you have a stroke, you're forced down paths that are uncomfortable; paths your nature didn't choose. I picture a community of stroke survivors as an island of misfit toys who commonly understand that there is no understanding. I see remarkable traits in what makes others "out of sync," and a beautiful fortitude in facing a newly forged path. Others see change and retreat in fear.

I'm a better person now than I once was. My faith is stronger. My priorities run deeper. In a world where the naturally "wired" lack solutions to some of the greatest questions we face, circumstance has forced me open to new perspective, and has introduced me to a world of phenomenal people, coping with new truths. I don't need to be understood to know that I'm not broken… I'm reborn. My stroke wasn't my downfall. It was my renaissance.

Renaissance

Forged within a fire, I never would have chosen,
Tangled up in lessons so obscenely interwoven,
Thrust before an alter that claimed a former life,
Steeped in a confusion, where desperation's rife.

Backward bent in chaos, with nowhere else to go,
Revelations challenging all I used to know.
Unwilling, and engulfed in fear, emerging from the haze,
Eyes adjusting from the fog and seeing truthful ways.

Breathing in, the air that burns; my lungs adjusting, strong,
A bright light that assaults my eyes, guiding me along.
The first step that I take along a path that is unknown,
A stumbling fawn approaching what is meant to be my own.

As born in grace, I head toward a path of understanding,
Compassion overwhelms my soul; my depth of life, expanding,
A renaissance of fancy flight; emerging faith and beauty,
Embraced by God, and nurtured whole, in purpose, love and duty.

I have not fallen. This life of mine, is not the worlds to claim.
Risen with divine reflection, I'll never be the same.
Wild spirit, carefree mind, no worldly force can tame.

I keep telling myself that tomorrow, I'll do better. I'll force myself to strength, rather than succumbing to weakness. But tomorrow never comes. It's logical to stay in bed when you're healing. But, at what point do you need to turn that around and recognize that you're not sleeping for recovery anymore? You're sleeping because it's easier than doing the work and facing the life that tried to claim you? All indications say that the moment you're present enough to ask that question, is the moment when it's time to get up.

That moment has come for me. While I may be limited in what pain and exhaustion allow me to achieve, it's time for me to set some limits around what pain and exhaustion are allowed to keep from me. Logical limits. It may keep me from running a marathon, but not from walking through a city to explore what's there. Perhaps brain fog will prevent me from devouring the writings of Tolstoy in a weekend, but I can savour a good plot over time. Chances are, I'm not going to acquire worthwhile degrees through an advanced, fast-paced curriculum, but I can and will learn meaningful information and skills at a pace my mind and body can accept.

I think it's pretty common to emerge from a stroke with new priorities and expectations. I don't know if it's the same for everyone, but for me, my new priorities coincide with my new capabilities. I don't want to run the marathon anymore. I want to walk slowly, absorbing everything around me. The prize is the action and the time, not the medal at the end. I want to think about a story and take the time to anticipate it. I want what I learn to matter in both my own life and the lives of others.

Up I get! Do I believe that I will occasionally revert back to my healing slumber? Absolutely. I'm only human. But I'm a human with God on my side. So, I will pray, and I will rise above the guilt of my failures and get up again. Isaiah 41:10 says "Fear not, for I am with you; be not dismayed, for I am your God; I will strengthen you, I will help you, I will uphold you with My righteous right hand." Words of encouragement over thousands of years, and the faith in my heart that tells me it's true.

It's Time

No time for excuses.

No tolerance for grief.
No failure I can't overcome,
Covered in belief.

There is no reason good enough,
To stop the upward motion;
No doubt ensnaring deep within;
Unconscious, blind commotion.

A mind of introspection,
A body that awakens,
Should focus on the beauty,
That trauma hasn't taken.

It's time to rise,
To recognize,
The duty of my skill,
And find inside,
A certain stride,
And life-defining will.

∞∞∞

Spasticity didn't strike me initially. I think one of the harder things to accept after stroke is that new symptoms can continue to occur for months after the primary event. That's a tough pill to swallow when you've already faced an initial smackdown that was absolutely crippling. The hope is always that there's nowhere to go but up.

It was about three months after my stroke that I started feeling pain in my legs, hips and back. It was about four months after that I had to admit that the pain was different from the chronic pain I've known for most of my life. It was five months when I accepted that the tightness and cramping that seemed like "Charley horses" in new areas; or what felt like something that could only be described as "early onset Rigor Mortis," was a part of my new reality that I'd need to learn how to manage.

Spasticity is neurological. It's a pretty common occurrence for those who have had a stroke, to experience involuntary muscle contractions because the brain is damaged in ways that make it unable to control muscular action. It can start almost immediately after the stroke, or months later, and it's not a condition that you can ignore without consequence. Deterioration will continue and pain will get worse without the work of stretching exercises and the commitment to maintain mobility. Often, people need medication, Botox injections and even surgeries, to alleviate the pain. I'm committed to the physical efforts to try to prevent the need for further intervention.

God has provided me with all of the tools necessary to reach a level of recovery that is seemingly miraculous. At the moment, I'm feeling a tightness and heaviness not conducive of a "well-oiled machine." It's time for me to learn the art of maintenance, in gratitude for this phenomenal body that I've been gifted. A body that can repair and re-wire itself; that can get up after it collapses, and that houses a mind of ingenious problem-solving techniques, and a will to power it forward.

Unrelenting

It never stops.
It never should.
For all that's worthy, strong and good,
Emerges, as a Phoenix would,
In ash, the warrior withstood.

I feel the pain.

I breathe it in.
A sign of life is found within,
And from there I cry out again;
The place where faith and hope begins.

It does not give to weaker way,
Or tortured minds that go astray,
Until, submissively, you pray,
"God, carry all my woes away,
And show my soul the light of day."

There's a general idea that an abundance of knowledge is among the most valuable tools that a person can possess. I question the validity of that in regard to strokes. Because the symptoms can be so diverse, and so much is unknown, I think that reading too much about them can result in getting stuck in your own head. I read online that, for women, hiccups can be a symptom of stroke. I don't doubt that claim, but if you're a stroke survivor, I'm sure that you understand the proclivity to question every single tingle and twinge that you feel as being related to your primary event. The more I become conscious of how often I do that, the more I come to realize how paralyzing it can be. For that reason, I regret having the knowledge that hiccups can be a symptom of stroke. In some ways, I yearn for blissful ignorance.

It's a trap; focusing so deeply on symptoms and challenges. The added stress one puts on himself/herself doing that, could age the healthiest of people and cause a decline in the general wellbeing of anyone. One can't ignore the challenges of stroke. But I think a number of us need to stop looking for more. It's possible that I just have hiccups because I ate my comfort food too quickly, and it's not a result of brain damage. Sometimes a headache is just stress.

Occasionally, a cramp is just because I slept in the wrong position, and nausea occurs for reasons like food choices.

Life goes on, and it shouldn't be continued inside the realm of fear and defeat for an indefinite period of time. I'm not going to seek out the world's tallest, shakiest roller coaster with strobe lights throughout, shots before boarding and a calming cigarette at the end. But I'm not going to deny myself the absolute thrill of a jet ski on open water, or a swig of Tuscan red on the rare occasion.

There's a difference between living life and existing in it. God didn't keep me here so that I could simply exist.

Balance

Lift your head from looking down,
Opportunity abounds;
A world that brims with sights and sounds,
Where life springs forth from fertile ground.

Take a breath; absorb it all,
Recognizing nature's call.
Release yourself from self-made walls,
And feel your prison start to fall.

Step with caution on sure feet,
Ignore the fear that begs retreat.
Remember times that once were sweet,
And made you joyfully complete.

Find within the passion lost,
Know the risk is worth the cost,
Lay it at Creation's door,
And live beyond what came before.

Find the balance that you seek;

A will that's strong when body's weak,
Bravely open, firmly bold;
You're capable of grit untold.

Five months after my stroke, I was faced with a challenge that called to be met with both tolerance and resilience. An ice storm hit my county, causing devastation that I have not seen in my community in my lifetime. Multiple cities were entirely without power. Downed trees and branches filled yards and parks and streets. Basements flooded and homes quickly dropped to freezing temperatures, with no restoration for days. My home is two separate apartments. My elderly mother lives in the upstairs apartment and my daughter and I live in the downstairs apartment. With the ice and rain continuing to fall, the three of us started bailing water from the sump to try to avoid flooding.

My daughter, though generally in good health, was ill at the time with a sore throat and congestion. My mother, prone to arthritis and sciatica, pushed through the pain. I, complaining often about the discomfort of spasticity, kept going until I fell into a wall from exhaustion, then I got up and continued. Together, we bailed for twenty-eight hours, with one of us on a four-hour break at all times. After twenty-eight hours, we had nothing left. We ran to remove the things we valued from bottom shelves, and we committed our home to God's hands. The rain stopped. We watched the water rise in our sump to within a quarter inch of the floor, and it stopped. It sat there for days, as our home became too cold to stay in, but remained dry.

Outside looked apocalyptic. Downed trees and branches on houses and cars, filling streets and properties. Hanging power lines were everywhere. It was shocking to see. Everyone began the long job of cleaning up as our city declared a state of emergency. Then, a few days later, we received notice of a severe weather watch. Another ice storm was on its way. I loaded my family into our car, emptied my bank account, and drove an hour north to buy a small used generator from someone. They had become hard-to-find commodities. We secured the generator and a can of gas and rushed back home just as the storm was starting. In the rush and stress of the moment, I foolishly didn't ask the seller to start it up in front of me, and when we got home, it didn't work. That night, my little basement apartment flooded. The comforts of home rotted under a foot of water, and I watched the routine I had established for stroke recovery, float away. No more quiet amidst the emotions that overwhelm me. No more feeling accomplished in achieving a balanced home on my own. No more heated bed or massage chair in the corner.

It's only "things." I repeated to myself how grateful I was to have my family safe and warm. "It's only things and things aren't what matters. The safety of my family is what matters." But in truth, it was quite hard to see, as my soggy life got torn up, thrown into a bin, and hauled away.

Tomorrow

The challenge of your hardest days,
As things dissolve in tragic ways,
Dulled silver lines clouds drenched in greys,
Emboldened by your prayers and praise,
A gratitude that roots and stays,
Though heavy on your soul, it weighs.

Be warm amidst God's safe embrace.
Find comfort in a threatening place,
As what you've known is laid to waste,

But what you find is depth in grace.

For things don't bind you to this life,
And blessings of your heart, entice,
Calling you to a gratitude,
And meek and simple attitude.

God save you from the tragic sphere,
Of loss and overwhelming fear,
And make your path to peace so clear,
You stride in confidence from here.

You have not lost. You're not defeated.
Though weary, with your will depleted,
Rise in faith and shed your sorrow,
With courage built to thrive tomorrow.

I think it was twelve days that we were without power from the initial ice storm. They successfully restored power to our local recreation facility to turn it into a relief centre, where people could go to get warm, recharge their phones and get a meal, since freezers and refrigerators in everyone's homes were full of melted, rotting food. There were cots set up so people could stay overnight. But my family has a dog and, after the second ice storm, she was freezing too. We slept at home for as long as our many blankets would allow, and then we checked into a hotel room at a local hotel that had just had power restored. I checked us in for two nights, but a clerical error switched it to one night, and we got kicked out the next day. With nothing left available in our city, we ventured a half hour away to another pet-friendly hotel. Sadly, it wasn't terribly friendly to me, as my allergies in that room flared to a point where it was a challenge to breathe and I was afraid to go to sleep.

After one night at that hotel, a friend of mine reached out. She and her family had been trapped inside their home for a couple of days by fallen trees, and the mess they had to clean from the storm was overwhelming. But, having gotten power back the previous night, she invited my family, dog and all, to stay in her basement for a couple of days, until they would have to return to work, and their own animals wouldn't be able to cope with our presence in their absence. It's not easy to accept help from a friend. But we were lost, and devoid of solutions, and genuinely moved to be cared for that much. When I count my blessings, I count that friend twice, because her heart is bigger than average, her mind stronger, and her shoulders can bear a weight greater than most.

After a couple of nights at my friend's house, with our power still out, and our dog still in tow, we pushed further from home for a place where we could sleep, cook a meal and do some laundry. Because of my allergies, laundromats are not an option. But, a condo in Toronto with an apartment sized washer/dryer was. For two nights, we lived a charming little lifestyle in the big city. We got clean. We refreshed. Then, we headed home to our newly restored power, and the chaos of recovery.

Jen

How blessed I am, in beauty fine,
To see a world that's so divine,
To know the kindness of my peers,
That see me through unwieldy fears,
Who give to me a million reasons,
To feel the faith inside me deepen.

Beyond a depth you feel with friends,
A hope for goodness, God intends,

To sweep this world, and so revealing,
The light self-interest is concealing,
With altruism; charity,
Sincere in generosity.

A glimpse of hope when beaten down,
A friendly face when none were found,
That opened up my eyes to see,
A world of warmth surrounding me.

I want to be the open soul,
Who offers righteousness in whole;
To give of comfort when I'm weary,
Build light for others when it's dreary.

I praise my God for sending me,
A friend who so inspires me.

The other night, I was out with my daughter for a long drive. We got off the highway, and there, on the overpass, my daughter pointed out a man holding a cardboard sign as he stood out in the cold. The sign read "I've had a stroke. Please help me." I wanted to sprint across lanes of traffic, swoop him up and take him to warmth and safety. Where would that be? My daughter is sleeping on our couch and our floors are flooded with boxes of what was salvaged from our flood. That could be me; watching cars breeze past me as my world falls apart. The presence of God in my life doesn't excuse me from the challenges and tragedies that build character and test faith. I'm embarrassed that it takes something so close to home to draw my attention to the tragic plight of others. Struggle doesn't make me unique. It makes me human. The better human that I want to be will give more time to the struggles of others than to my own.

God has shown me grace. He has built my resilience and restructured my priorities. He has taught me with depth and distinction that, my effort and actions matter deeply, but my life is not mine to control and the world will spin on the axis of His choosing. He has also taught me that my outlook and attitude can affect, not only my reality, but that of those around me.

In the moment that we saw the man on the overpass, I feared that I had nothing to offer him. But, that's not true. I'm committed to return to that place and if I see him there, I will aspire to help. I will feed him. I will offer words of empathy in a spirit of faith and love. I can't house him, but I can make a day of his life a little easier. If I can fill my life with countless days that embrace that purpose, I will be a success. I pray that God gives me the strength and motivation to do so from any circumstance life presents me with.

My Teacher

I didn't see your struggle.
I didn't feel your pain.
Clothed in willful blindness,
Priorities I deigned,
Found worth in being vain.

I never set my focus on the value of your plea,
Never contemplated the courage of humility,
Or the soul's prosperity.

Character is forged in fire,
Endeavouring in battles, dire,
When through the war, our hearts grow tired,
But we rise, triumphantly inspired.

I see you now, through clearer eyes.
With empathy, I realize,
You are not poor in values measured,
You are my teacher, deeply treasured.

I recently had someone ask me "what would you want to do with your life if you had no physical limitations?" I didn't have an answer. I suppose my mind has not entertained that as a possibility. While it's not an answer I seemed likely to arrive at quickly, the question itself made me want to test my limits. What might I be capable of if I pushed until my tank was empty? Would God carry me from there? Would I be reminded once again that control isn't mine? Would the exercise of trying lead me to submit the stress of the effort to God for a token of faith?

Two days after being asked that fateful question, I received a call from Elections Canada. I had worked many elections in the past, and they were short on Supervisors for the upcoming election. There was no time to question it or worry about it. The challenge was an eight-hour day of training the day after they called and a work day of at least fifteen hours two days after that. Talk about a leap of faith. I struggle deeply with post-stroke fatigue. How long could the adrenaline from a challenge carry me through? Would God sustain me for the virtue of my effort? It was time to find out.

I set out to prove to myself that I could work a 15-hour day, doing something that required use of my brain. The majority of stroke recovery happens within the first six months. Having just crossed that threshold, I needed to feel capable. I was hired as a Central Poll Supervisor on standby (not assigned to any poll.) After three hours at the main election office, I was dispatched to a poll location that was overwhelmed. I relieved long lines. I balanced ballot counts of multiple polls that others struggled with. I answered questions of all levels of workers. I was praised endlessly for being so helpful. Does it sound like I'm bragging? … because I am! My day started slowly and moved me around in ways that didn't drain on me in one intense drive, but utilized my skills and knowledge in various types of work to help others through. I paced myself. It wasn't the day I had planned. It was a day God planned for me, to allow me to feel the absolute success of my effort. Six months post-stroke, I completed a 15-hour, 40-minute day. I was barely able to move the next day. It took me until 3pm to successfully get from my bed to the couch, and I headed back to bed very shortly after. But I reconciled that if it took me a week to recover from one day, I would continue to focus on that one day… because I was awesome, and capable and bright, and God gave me that day to fully know it.

What would I want to do with my life if I had no physical limitations? I'd want to hand it over to a wiser, loving, higher power, because I can't even fathom the capabilities and plans that He has for me. I just know they're always greater than I anticipate.

What Might I Do?

The realm of possibilities is endless in His sight,
The boundless ways I measure my solitary might,
I build in strength and comfort, unfathomable light,
And toss my anguish in the flames, knowing faith is right,

What might I do if I submit my future to His hand,
But cease to feel the struggle of treading in the sand,
And open to a feeling of peace I understand,
Engulfed in wild brilliance of the life that God has planned?

His world is greater than I see.

His concepts wise and deep and free,
And I could live to always be,
The greatest parts that fashion me.

Is Heaven sought for streets of gold?
For pearly gates and wealth untold?
Or is it built by what unfolds,
In sacrifice, of heart so bold?

I offer up the best of me,
And work in true integrity,
In thanks for every day I wake,
And each and every breath I take.

What might I do? What could I be?
But heaven-bound, in nature, free.

Many years ago, I saw this story on television that moved me in a way that has stayed with me to this day. It was about a man named Nicholas Winton. He had successfully saved 669 children from the horrors of Nazi invasion in Prague, just before Hitler moved into Czechoslovakia. This televised moment was one of the most moving things I had ever seen. They sat Mr. Winton in the front row of the studio audience and began talking about the scrapbook of records he had compiled of the many children he liberated, then introduced him to the woman next to him, who was one of those children. The host then asked if there was anyone else in the audience who owed their lives to Mr. Winton, would they please stand up. The entire audience stood. They had filled the studio with lives that man had saved. I researched him a little. He was a remarkable man who sought no praise for his achievements. But, for me, the most stunning thing about him was the motto by which he lived... "If something's not impossible, there must be a way of doing it."

Imagine if we all lived by that motto. Day after day, I read the stories and struggles of stroke survivors. I see the questions and the fears. The hopeless tones overwhelm me at times. Then, I read the story of a warrior; one who finds deep purpose and overcomes the despair. "If something's not impossible, there must be a way of doing it." That beautiful statement is the epitome of faith. Faith in God. Faith in yourself. Faith in creation to provide a path.

My stroke hasn't limited my possibilities. It has simply forced me to find another direction. If I want to move forward in life; find purpose and passion, I only need faith and effort. With that, I could liberate myself, and countless others, just as Mr. Winton did.

There Must Be a Way

When overwhelmed by deep despair,
With no clear path to take from there,
When burdened by a crushing weight,
And challenged by oppressive fate,
What's possible from disarray;
The faith that there must be a way.

With knowledge gone and comfort lost,
On paths we've never dared to cross,
Reluctant in our own ambition,
Starving for a vague volition,
Fearful in the light of day,
But mindful, there must be a way.

When crying out to nature "why?"
And begging God to hear your cry;
To answer to your angered plea,

"How could you let this conquer me?"
You listen close and hear Him say
"Arise, My child. There is a way."

In God, nothing's impossible,
And faith can move all things
And in this realm of trial,
And the challenges it brings,
Confused and taken from your path,
Bow your head and pray.
If something's not impossible,
Than God must have a way,
And in the faith of chosen souls,
He'll guide you there one day.

The more tired I get, the more my scalp feels like it's on fire. Prior to my stroke, I'd have found that unusual. Now, I passively accept it as normal in my abnormal world. I also find moderate amusement in the fact that my dad's nickname, up until he passed just a few years ago, was "Torch." I used to look for similarities between us. Never had I considered varying forms of "hot heads."

I've looked up my flaming scalp online, which seems to have largely overtaken the itchy sensation that was so prevalent for some time. The most reasonable match I've found was something called "Central Post-Stroke Pain." It's described as a neuropathic pain that happens because the stroke may have affected the brain's processing centres. Much like its predecessor (and occasional recurring visitor,) "The Itch," it seems rooted in the same cause, and it's not something I discuss much with my doctor. That's largely because the allopathic treatments used aren't something I'm open to taking in order to cope with my occasional moderately painful annoyance.

I'm learning to listen to my body, as it gives less than subtle hints as to my correct path. It's alright to rest when I'm tired. There's value in trying to treat uncomfortable symptoms with various foods and supplements. While their counsel is worthy of deep consideration and genuine gratitude, not all answers come from a physician. Sometimes, the experiences of your community carry the knowledge and strength that you need to overcome an issue of adversity. Occasionally, your own exploration opens pathways to learning and developing the coping strategies that you need. But among the vast toolkit that I've accepted as my way forward, nothing surpasses that of my faith. Beyond medicine and community and physical therapy and alternative healing, there is God; a spirit of purpose that elevates me. A knowledge that, absent of power, I grow in charity and compassion, not just for others, but for myself.

Yours

Heal me with pain.
With the feeling of summiting the insurmountable as I cry out claims of weakness, from which You raise me up.

Cessate my mental anguish with knowledge that seemingly overwhelms my capacity.

Feed my spirit to know a growth beyond what my heart can abide, or what my soul can accept.

Teach me - not just through lessons and example, but through the blistering fire of experience.

And, when I look to You, exhausted and defeated, float me as a feather in ethereal grace... not to wisdom or strength or greatness, but to be Yours.

∞∞∞

I can't count the number of times I've read the question from others "Do we ever recover from a stroke?" The answer is no. Stroke isn't something that you recover from. The part of you that dies doesn't spring back to life again. You don't return to who you were. But with strength and resilience, through the grace of God, you can rise to something greater.

When you see how fragile and precious life is, you value it. When faced with a genuine threat to your well-being, deeper priorities form. With the loss of some abilities, you realize how very blessed you are to have those that remain, and you find strength in the pursuit of developing new pathways for others.

Stroke isn't about recovery. It's about transformation. It's about re-wiring. It's about something new, uncomfortable and important. It's not for the weak. It's a battle for a warrior. It can lead to solitude and unfamiliar surroundings. Without a firm grasp on the Creator, it can devastate your mind and heart. For me, it wasn't a leap into faith. My stroke was a push into faith, that the old me wasn't strong enough to consent to. It was absolutely necessary for my growth, and absolutely devastating to so much of what I embraced. God saved me for a purpose. He rebuilt me with the tools I need to achieve something meaningful. That's not how it felt when I laid in the hospital, broken and confused. It's my reality now because I leaned into Him and sought answers. I'm not recovered. I'm remade.

Re-made

Brick-by-brick...
A foundation from which a phoenix can soar.

Put aside what used to be.
Remake the very heart of me.
Shift my path to something new,
And teach me things I never knew.

Ever-growing in peace and mind.
I set what has passed on an alter, in sacrifice to what can be.

You will not watch as I recover,
But see me bloom into another,
With gratitude in every step,
And nary room for old regret.

With passion for my own being, my Creator overwhelms me.
To be made... and remade.

What value sweet I must possess;
The blessed gift to once progress.
I needn't hold my yesterday,
For I have found a better way.

I don't like the rain. It's dreary and heavy and it makes my heart sink a bit. It makes it terribly ironic that I seem to find comfort in storms now. Perhaps it's a level of acceptance of the knowledge that I'm not in control. Maybe it's the low growl of thunder that makes me feel like the earth is speaking to me. Whatever the source of my general ease, I watch the lightening and hear the pounding rain, and I know how small the noise within me is by comparison. My own little world could feel like it's burning to the ground in a fevered nightmare, but that fire will never burn big enough to light up the whole sky and make it crash and boom in protest. Whatever turmoil stirs within me, is a whimper by comparison. If God can control the heavens, in thunderous chorus, and wrap it all up with a rainbow, I feel confident that I don't present much of a challenge to His abilities.

The things that happen in my life aren't insignificant. They deeply affect both me and others. They ripple into the lives of those around me, causing concern or elation, depending on the source. They set a tone and rhythm for either calm or storm. I've come to the realization that both are valuable and necessary. I still panic when internal lightening strikes. But as my life progresses amidst my re-wired thoughts and priorities, I move closer to understanding that sunbeams are most impressive when they break through the darkest clouds. That contrast creates incredible beauty, and both the dark and the light, are God-sent.

The Sound of Thunder

The crack of thunder, bold and loud;
The heaven's anger cried aloud.
The lighted skies so brightly play,
With all its corners on display.

The thunder shouts. I know its rage.
My naked soul on spotlit stage.
And growing fast and wildly,
A storm that brews inside of me.

I look above, with brightened eyes,
Beyond the threat of thunderous skies,
As pounding rain in rhythmic beat,
Lays waste to chaos and defeat.
The face of God, my spirit meets.

In ever-burdened, panicked thought,
That solitary motion brought,
Releasing bright and booming pain,
Conducted in my own refrain.

Above the clouds, my storm, I lift,
As faith and knowledge start to shift,
Submitting what I can't control,
And finding peace, alive and whole.

Thunder cracks to mask my shout,
While lightening blinds my failures out,
And rain, it washes all away,
As sunbeams break to better days,
Of mercy, hope and words of praise.

I think that having a stroke leaves one prone to visualizing incremental goals. I'm trying to break down the value in that. Recently, I heard someone articulate a fairly common long-term goal. "I'm going to live to be one hundred years old." I thought about that a lot. Initially, my thoughts were about my next goal… "I'm going to live to be forty-seven, at least." But, the more I think about it, the more I find myself shifting the emphasis of that statement. "I'm going to LIVE. And, whatever age I live to, I'm going to be satisfied with the quality of who I am and what I achieve." That's the goal. That's what I need to find a path to. Not a number or milestone, but a commitment to inspiration and development. What a terrifying thought. I'm physically hurt. Reaching forty-seven really felt challenging enough.

I don't know how people manage without faith; carrying the

weight of the world without an all-powerful support system. It's why I read so many stories of defeated people. They're not striving for one-hundred, or for forty-seven. They're just trying to find a reason to get out of bed in the morning. What happens to your body as a result of stroke, is beyond difficult. But what can happen to your soul can be crushing and devastating.

Perhaps the value in incremental goals is in the details and the character one finds in slow motion and appreciation. Maybe the reason to get up is for nothing more than to brew a coffee to help fuel your next step. For some, it may be smaller than that. Learn to move a finger again. Eventually, it will flip the switch on the coffee maker. Anything that requires focus and effort, builds us. It makes us stronger. It builds our gratitude and spirit. The amount of opportunity that exists from fighting your way from finger movement to coffee-making to one hundred years old, is what legends are made of. Created in the image of One who created all, imagine what you could achieve. Submitting your conscience to the will of that Creator, can lift the limits of your own perceptions. Get out of bed in the morning. You're not finished. You've only just begun.

Live

Is life a physical activity or a state of mind?
If fear can cripple you, surely faith can raise you up.

To cower in the face of forward motion...

I may fall.
I may see the reflection of my own weaknesses.
I may fail.
But I will live.

It's not existence that I crave.

The sweet taste of fruit doesn't feed my soul.
My senses; mere physical manifestations of being...

Touch that hints at how deeply I can feel.

Sounds of song and comfort to bring peace - or of anger and confusion to motivate me.

My eyes have bathed in phenomenal beauty that my physical mind could not fathom.
Grey and dust to an enlightened spirit.

The smell of nature, fresh and clean, invites me to connect with what's pure.

I am alive.

Once breath and flesh and bone.
I existed.

Now, in faith, hope and love,
I live.

I'd love to be able to tell you that you're never going to hit a wall in your progress. That life is sunshine and roses and there's nowhere to go but up. The difficult truth is, progress is always going to take effort, and I've never met a single person who aligns physically, spiritually and mentally 100% of the time.

You can know that God is there and on your side, and still fall into that pit you didn't notice was at your feet. You can still hit that barrier that life violently thrusts in your path, that's so tall and so wide, you can't fathom it having an end.

When that happens to me, I've found it most uplifting to remind myself of two things. The first is that, with God, all things are possible. He is in control, and He doesn't want me to fail. He wants me to succeed. If the path is difficult, He wants me to succeed triumphantly, and He has built an in road to that triumph. The other thing is, everything has an end. The seemingly endless and insurmountable barrier, does have edges, and I'll never find them by standing in the same place and straining my eyes. That's a difficult understanding to overcome when you feel like your feet are in quicksand. But there is a way. "If something's not impossible, then there must be a way to do it." That way is faith. Belief. A faith in God. A belief in yourself and your phenomenal function as a human being.

God built us with reason and strength and incredible ability to create and innovate and solve problems. He fashioned our bodies in such a way that we can repair ourselves... re-wire and take on new initiatives. A blind person often finds a heightening of his/her other senses. One of the most brilliant minds of the last century, Stephen Hawking, was confined to a wheelchair and unable to speak without technological assistance. Within each of us is the potential for a spark of divinity. Ignite it!

Mine

When nature exhales, I breathe in.
Where waters rush, my flow begins.
Where treetops sway, I dance in time,
For all this world is wholly mine.

There's nothing that I can't achieve.
I bring to life what I believe.
And faced with tense and soulful woe,
The mired soil at my toe,
I plant my feet and start to grow.

I see no boundary great enough,
To hinder where I go;
No force beyond me, I can't slough;
No victory I can't know.

Created in the image of One who is divine,
This world is my inheritance, woven deep and fine.
No binding can restrain me from what God says is mine.

∞∞∞

I started writing when I was young. At first, it was a way to understand myself. What I couldn't sort through in thought or speech, flowed onto paper, and when I read it back, it was pristinely me. As I developed an interest in poetic expression, I would find individual words that would stir some emotion in me. I suppose it was indicative of the beauty I see within language. Over time, the rhythm of a poem began to feel like a heartbeat to my thoughts. The rhyme, a whimsical song. Every word that came from me, held meaning to me. I was odd. Quirky. I suppose I still am. But, as a child, it was a barrier to my confidence, and I had no means of connecting who I was, with others. Writing and poetry were the purest expression of me.

When I had my stroke, I lost those things. My ability to write. The connection of my thought and my words. I couldn't type a coherent sentence and I was terrified. My basic tools and greatest way to connect with others, vanished. I didn't know if they'd come back. The logic that remained amidst much confusion told me that part of my brain had died. Death isn't something one recovers from. But, over the course of my recovery, I've learned just how phenomenal God built us to be.

After a stroke, there's much one has to re-learn. Many lessons have a solid foundation already in place, but new pathways to success in life's simplest things, have to be developed. As part of you passes, new parts spring to life in an effort to compensate. Re-wired to bypass what you've lost, you begin the out-of-body, out-of-sync process of doing everything in a different way than what your brain had initially chosen as its most effective method. It's hard. It's frightening. It's exhausting. But, in it is a possibility for growth and new priorities, and maybe even an exploration of new strengths.

I've always looked at the intricacies of this world in awe. The human body and spirit, and its symbiotic connection to all that surrounds us, have always served as absolute proof of a higher power to me. God made people in His image. That was clear. But, on October 23rd, 2024, for some reason, He began the process of remaking me. What had I done with the first phase of my life that was worthy of a second round? What would I do with this next phase of my life that could serve a greater purpose than the last? Re-wired once again to express my thoughts and emotions with new priorities, I prayed that I might find the words to write to the glory of God, and inspire others by doing so.

My journey to finding faith through the challenges of stroke recovery, continues. When I first put pen to paper while laying in my hospital bed, the effort began as therapy. That therapy has evolved over time. From gibberish my mind couldn't sort to the deep expression of God's influence on my life, and the overwhelming gratitude I cling to amidst vivid knowledge of what I once took for granted.

I have my words back. I have the ability to communicate with my daughter back. I have a wit to make others laugh, and a passion to plan incredible things. Whatever God intends for me moving forward, He didn't hook me up this well for nothing. My future is promising. My recovery is remarkable. My faith is unending.

May you find faith that brings you peace and mercy that reveals your direction.

Made in the USA
Columbia, SC
20 June 2025